The Evolution of the Black Rifle:

20 Years of Upgrades, Options, and Accessories

by

Jeff Zimba

Dystopian Fiction & Survival Nonfiction

www.PrepperPress.com

The Evolution of the Black Rifle: 20 Years of Upgrades, Options, and Accessories

ISBN 978-0692317266

Copyright © 2014 by Jeff Zimba

Front cover image of Jeff Zimba: 2013, Smoking Gun Photography

Back cover image: 2012, James Brown

Printed in the United States of America.

Prepper Press Trade Paperback Edition: November 2014

Prepper Press is a division of Kennebec Publishing, LLC

Table of Contents

About the Author

Jeff W. Zimba was introduced to firearms at an age too young to remember. He recalls, "My father and grandfather used to enjoy target shooting and reloading between big game hunting seasons. I used to tag along with them on their many trips to the range, and as you can imagine, it was difficult to record data and focus on fine tuning with a curious and talkative young man in the midst of things. To keep me quiet and safely entertained, they would blow up a bag of balloons and staple their necks to a big sheet of plywood on an impact area ninety degrees from theirs, so we could sit together but shoot safely in different directions. I was given a few boxes of .22LR, a rifle or pistol, and told to let the adults shoot and focus on popping all the balloons. It was an exercise I looked forward to, every trip to the range."

Ten days after graduating from high school, Zimba reported for duty in the United States Navy at Great Lakes, Illinois, with the dream of a career. Unfortunately, an injury quickly had him packing his sea bag and heading back home for surgery. With no plans for further education and no other job prospects, he started a retail gun shop and became an NFA firearms manufacturer. It was the largest retail NFA-stocking gun shop in the state for several years. It was at that point that he found he had a knack for breaking things from extreme use, which always necessitated fixing, and occasionally improving, the original system. He started keeping notes on all the data he collected and eventually started spending more time on the shooting range than in the store.

After a short stint working with Long Mountain Outfitters, a large Type 10 (Manufacturer of Destructive Devices) wholesale dealer, importer, and manufacturer, he was on the ground level in starting a new magazine Small Arms Review primarily covering NFA firearms (machineguns, sound suppressors, destructive devices, short-barreled rifles, shotguns, etc.) and served as the production manager and staff writer for over fifteen years, specializing in articles on the testing and evaluation of systems both new and old. He continued to assist manufacturers in research and development on new designs, and continues to be active in the industry to this day.

His articles have been published in several countries in numerous gun magazines including Machine Gun News – USA, Small Arms Review Magazine – USA, Shotgun News – USA, The American Rifleman – USA, AK-47 & Soviet Weapons Annuals – USA, ARMI Magazine – Germany, PLATOON Magazine – South Korea, and several others.

These days, Zimba remains a freelance writer and maintains a Firearms T&E YouTube Channel (www.YouTube.com/Bigshooterist) to share new information. He is the CEO of Small Arms Research, a New England-based firearms test facility, and he works closely with several manufacturers of firearms, ammunition, and accessories in research and development. He is a longtime activist for the Second Amendment on the state and federal levels and enjoys his time in the Maine woods and waters as a licensed Master Maine Guide, focusing primarily on providing outdoor opportunities for combat wounded veterans. He is an active firearms instructor, working with all levels of shooting, and enjoys "sharing the craft" with new shooters the most. He continues learning at every opportunity, considering himself a "perpetual Student of the Gun" with years of study ahead. In his "spare time" he appears on the hit reality television shooting show "Freedom Fighters," airing on the Pursuit Channel.

Visit www.BigShooterist.com to learn more about Jeff Zimba.

Dedications and Acknowledgements

This book represents almost twenty years of testing and evaluation. It is just a small part of the body of testing I have done and only pertains to one specific system. None of this could have been accomplished without the following people:

My Father and Grandfather – Had you not lit the candle that ignited my interest in firearms into the inferno it is today, this may be a book titled *Corvettes*, or maybe *How to Survive an Economic Depression with No Leadership or Responsibility in Government*, or *100 Ways to Know Your Elders are MUCH Smarter than You Ever Thought You Were Growing Up*.

Thank you both dearly.

My Wife – We're going on thirty years of my bringing guns home or leaving to go to the range, saying "This is all for work," and you letting me get away with it with a straight face. I promise I will stop improving the range temporarily, and build that new house soon. Really this time. Thank you for your patience.

My Son – Young man, you give me a reason to strive and do better at everything I do. My only mission at this point is to "pass it on" to you, so you may do the same with your kids. I know it is rough on you when I travel, but with a stiff upper lip you accept becoming "the man of the house" anyway. Thank you for your understanding and making me a better person.

My Military Brothers in Arms – It is your selfless dedication to this amazing experiment in freedom that continues to safeguard everything we hold sacred. Putting yourself in harm's way and spending countless nights "on their doorstep" so it need not come to ours, you are usually in great discomfort, when you would much rather be home, warm, and surrounded by your loved ones, is something I can never offer a sufficient "thanks" for. I'll try anyway... thank you for your service.

My Mentors and Friends in the Firearms Industry – It was the many conversations with the people I used to read about in my youth, including Max Atchisson, James Leatherwood, Dolf Goldsmith, and others that really let me know I was actually part of YOUR community. My dearly departed mentor and frequent traveling companion, William Vallerand, forgot more in his lifetime than I can ever hope to learn. Their passion for design and technology, history and function, improvement, development, and a calling, of sorts, to keep the craft alive by passing it on is the reason I look at everything differently and feel the same obligation to do the same. Thank you for your dedication and devotion to this industry.

Preface

Firearms are a way of life for millions of freedom-loving American families. From life and death self-defense considerations for citizens, law enforcement and military, to the definitive "aim small miss small" discipline of competition and safety, to the ubiquitous recreational use for hunting and casual plinking, firearms not only bring ultimate joy to our lives, but in millions upon millions of life threatening encounters, they protect life itself.

As a twenty-plus year Director of the Board for the mighty National Rifle Association and a lifetime "we the people" freedom fighter, this old guitar player's quality of life can be measured by the hours, days, weeks, years, and decades he has spent celebrating all things guns.

I have hunted my entire life, carried a gun on my person for more than forty-five years, have been an LEO for more than thirty years and have been privileged to train with the U.S. military warriors seemingly forever. Thoroughly tested firearms are imperative for all pragmatic and utilitarian considerations, and all the shootists I know truly value and rely upon the extensive testing and R&D that is responsible for the world class quality we have in firearms today.

My ballistic Blood Brother, Jeff Zimba, is right up there on the frontlines of such testing and torturing, and based on the sea of hot brass we more often than not find Jeff knee deep in, it would be difficult to find someone more experienced and dedicated to share the results of such quality control testing.

If the name Jeff Zimba is on a book, blog, column or article, you can rest assured that the tests are thorough, exhausting, comprehensive, creative, and believable. Jeff Zimba is the real McCoy, and I consider him my shootist Blood Brother.

Ted Nugent

Foreword

You could be forgiven for suspecting that a lot of the people who make a living writing about guns mostly grind out puff pieces in exchange for the free stuff given to them by the people who make the guns. Because … well, because it happens. We all know it. We all live with it. Or hope to. And it often happens – maybe even usually happens – without anyone having to say anything. Without even a nod or a wink. If you are the writer and say nice things, the free stuff will keep coming. If you are the producer and you send things to the right people, then the good words will keep on flowing. It is called "life."

In the civilian world, this means that some people own guns that they bought on the basis of bad information. They may be unhappy with what they bought. May even be let down, at the range or in the deer woods, by a product that they acquired on the basis of a recommendation that they wish they hadn't trusted. Unfortunate, but not fatal.

But those of us whose lives – and the lives of innocents around us – depend on the reliability and performance of the equipment we carry don't deal in minor disappointments and frustrations. When equipment fails, people can – and often do – die. And this is particularly true when the equipment that fails is a gun. It can ruin your entire day and spoil your whole mood.

So when it comes to our equipment – especially our weapons – we are inclined to ask a very simple question: Would you deploy with this tool when everything you know about it is based on promotional material put out by the manufacturer or some tame "gun critic" who is in that manufacturer's pocket?

The unsurprising answer is – I wouldn't, and neither would any of my teammates.

So we have our own strict testing requirements, administered by people who are in nobody's pocket. But we still appreciate the existence of a starting point – an outside evaluator who puts things through a punishing set of tests and then publishes the honest, unadorned truth about the results. Someone we can trust, the way we need to trust the equipment. Someone who gives us what we don't get in the glossy sales brochure handed out by the guy wanting to cap a lucrative deal on range day.

We are looking for something in the world of gun testing and evaluation that resembles what we used to do back in the days of the SEAL Team project called Red Cell. What we did at Red Cell was to take on the security of those bases and organizations that really needed to be secure. The kind where they had nuclear weapons in supposedly safe storage, or that held important communications equipment. The kind, in short, where if the security was breached, there would be very, very big problems. Maybe even for the whole world.

We didn't hold back. Compromise wasn't part of the mission. And we proved, over and over, that a guarantee that some base or facility was absolutely secure wasn't worth ... well, anything. We made a lot of people who issued that kind of guarantee very angry. But, hey, that was our job and we were very good at it.

Jeff Zimba has a similar kind of job and he is also very good at it. He tests many, many guns and accessories for a variety of markets and to say he tests them thoroughly and rigorously would be a vast understatement. He pushes and punishes the guns he tests way beyond the point of normal – and even abnormal — use. He often ends up in a pile of brass and links with what remains of a once new and highly hyped gun, pointing to the smoking and broken parts, and saying, "Don't do this at home or it will happen to you."

The kind of punishment he administers to a gun is brutal, as is the way he communicates about the results. What he publishes is not hype, meant to sell guns and keep him in good with the people who make them, but real information for people who really depend on the products he is testing. For people like that (like me) there is a value to this kind of service that is impossible to put a number on.

But we appreciate it, as will anyone reading the book you hold in your hands. This is the real deal. You can trust what you read here. And depend on it the same way you must depend on the tool you are using in situations where, if it doesn't work, the manufacturer's policy on returns won't make the slightest bit of difference.

Written by T. Daniel Capel, currently the CEO and President of Black Canyon Laboratories. Dan deployed six years in Afghanistan and three years in Iraq as a paramilitary officer, and is a former member of SEAL Team Six, and Red Cell.

Introduction

Si Vis Pacem Para Bellum – **If you desire Peace, Prepare for War.**

Looking through this small collection of articles I have penned over the last few decades, all in one place, immediately exemplified the very reason I thought this introduction was so important. As I flipped through the pages, looking over the initial draft, the years flew back into focus like a time machine. It didn't take long before I thought to myself, "Gosh, the times sure have changed a lot." Like generational changes in clothes, hairstyles, music, and dancing, so is the same for the firearms community. I remember being tutored by some well-known professional shooters in the mid-1980s and being told to get my strong hand elbow straight up to maximize stability. The school of thought has since changed greatly and correctly in my opinion, when shooting a full auto, to "tuck in" and make a smaller signature. Looking back at some of the older photos, they do look goofy, but certainly didn't at the time. Even weak hand holds have evolved several times, with the debate never ending on vertical or horizontal or even angled foregrips, and the latest "new" tactical and competitive hold is almost hyper extended as far toward the muzzle as safely possible. Being a simple "gun plumber" I don't create or design tactics, or even pretend to, but simply evolve as I learn. Who knows what will be next.

My job since the late 1980s has been testing and evaluating (T&E) firearms, usually those in the National Firearms Act (NFA) category. I have worked with several companies in the Research and Development (R&D) area as well, since a lot of trigger time helps to acclimate one to areas that may be problematic or easy to improve. As you will see in these pages, even though this book covers only one firearm, the AR-15/M16/M4/416 (and numerous other company specific designations), there have been several evolutions, changes, modifications and accessories. Some have taken off like a rocket and will be familiar and common, while others never really "stuck" and you may have never seen them before.

The information in these pages is a trip through time, looking over my shoulder as I have watched the industry change in relation to this amazing, modular weapon system. Because some of these writings were a few decades ago, and the companies or offerings may be long gone, the contact information has been removed to spare a new owner of an old number several uncomfortable conversations and/or messages. This body of work is not intended to be a buyer's guide, but simply a glimpse into the many changes that have been made.

While I have penned tens of thousands of words on other systems, makes, and models, the truth is, this beautiful black rifle remains this writer's favorite weapon system. Its modularity is unmatched by any other. From .22LR to 50BMG, the number of chambering options available is almost unlimited and continues to grow every day. It has been the top selling "Modern Sporting Rifle" (MSR) for several years and shows no sign of slowing down. With a single lower receiver you can own a fast, flat-shooting varmint rifle AND a great big game gun, capable of ethically dispatching any animal in North America, without even needing a single tool to convert. From the newly popular "pistol" versions with <8" barrels, to 24" H-BARs, there are fans for each configuration that justify a free market that can support new companies making their own specialty almost weekly.

When I purchased my first AR-15 in the 1980s it was a Colt, Model SP1. A virtually identical "sporter" to the first one sold by Colt since the 1960s. At that time, there were two options to a prospective purchaser, Colt or "Aftermarket." Colt made the most expensive and most desirable guns, with about a dozen smaller manufacturers offering the same gun, in varying qualities. Fast forward to the current day and there are over 300 companies offering versions of this now iconic design. The term "aftermarket" is a phrase of the past now, with some of the newer companies manufacturing the most desirable, and even most expensive offerings. The names are not limited to specialty companies making only black rifles these days either. Large companies including Remington, Sturm Ruger, High Standard, H&K, and many more join the ranks of POF-USA, BCI Defense, Troy Industries, and LWRC in making quality arms.

Though this collection of articles is now finalized between these covers, the T&E and R&D continues at a rapid pace. A second edition may be ready, with equal or greater content in less time, given the enormous number of "players" involved today. If you would like a peek into new technology being tested as this book goes to print, here are a few designs currently being evaluated that I believe may pass the test of time and eventually become commonplace:

- **POF-USA (Patriot Ordnance Factory) of Glendale, Arizona is making their 4th Generation of the P415 and P416 system. They recently introduced their E² (Esquared) Chamber.** In short, it is four small cuts or channels in the neck of the chamber that aid in extraction by utilizing the gas pressure previously sent out the bore. Though their research has been ongoing for quite some time, this new design is still somewhat unknown as it was only recently introduced.

- **Huntertown Arms "Dolos" Quick Change Barrel Takedown System**. While known typically for their sound suppressor line, this Indiana manufacturer has recently released the "Dolos" QD Barrel System. Appropriately named after the Greek God of deception or trickery, once installed, it allows the assembly or disassembly of any standard AR barrel with any standard AR upper receiver without tools, simply by rotating the handguard slightly. The Achilles heel of any QD barrel system is the ability to retain perfect zero after disassembly and reassembly and so far in this writer's experience, it is performing very well.

- **BCI Defense of Bremen, Indiana. Author's pick to watch for future advancements**. Out of all the newer manufacturers, it is tough to pick a single one who stands out from the pack. While there are numerous companies making some high quality rifles, I firmly believe that BCI Defense is a name we will all be familiar with in years to come. This is for many reasons, including, but not limited to the following: 1) Their parent company is a very successful, industry leading foundry with over 100 years in business. They make good decisions and have the ability to not only keep up with a changing industry, but be leaders in innovation. 2) The President and CEO are long-time enthusiasts of the AR platform with several years of using it. They are sensitive in diagnosing issues and identifying customer needs for an improved system in professional and recreational capacities. 3) BCI has a world-class manufacturing facility with the ability to manufacture almost every part of the system with quality control and "American Made" being a top priority. 4) BCI has assembled a team of people from very successful reaches of the AR industry with an amazing collective of experience.

I hope you enjoy this journey through the modern history and development of "The Black Rifle" and its many upgrades and accessories over the last few decades. It is an exciting time for this once greatly overlooked weapon system (and it is truly a "weapon system" with its amazing modularity) as it has gone from uncommon and obscure to the top-selling Modern Sporting Rifle in America in the last several years. The longest serving primary service rifle in United States Military history has finally received the attention in the civilian market it deserves.

The Evolution of the Modern Black Rifle

From Vietnam to the War on Terror
This Ever Changing Rifle System Continues to Evolve and Thrive

September 1, 1987. A Sea-Air-Land (SEAL) team member carries his Colt Commando assault rifle through the woods during a field training exercise. *(DoD photo by PHI Chuck Mussi)*

Every war is different. Every battleground has diverse characteristics. Each mission, whether a military role or civilian law enforcement detail varies greatly in its specific purposes. It seems almost impossible on the surface that a single weapon system could adapt and function in such a range of climates and missions, but the familiar M16 is still going strong. From a lightweight carbine to a heavy barreled LMG, the M16 weapon system has been fulfilling the role of America's primary service weapon for more than <u>40 years</u> and it doesn't seem it will be replaced wholesale anytime soon.

The earliest history of the inception and design of the black rifle bas been chronicled numerous times and it is not the intent of this author to rehash this historical material other than a very brief and condensed historical summary. There are many credible sources for this information including The Complete AR-15/M16 Sourcebook by Duncan Long, The Black Rifle I by Blake Stevens, Black Rifle II by Christopher R. Bartocci and an extensive Colt M16 ID Guide in the Machine Gun Dealers Bible by Dan Shea. This article will focus on the versatility of the M16, the characteristics that have allowed the metamorphosis from the original designs to the current battle rifle of the 21st century and possibly beyond.

Although there are a countless number of model designations for these rifles from numerous manufacturers, for simplicity purposes in this article, the designation "M16" can be assumed to be a fully automatic rifle while the designation "AR-15" makes reference to the semiautomatic version.

A Very Brief History

November 18, 1967. Marine grunts exit their transportation, a CH-53A Sea Stallion with Marine Heavy Helicopter Squadron 463, to begin a search and destroy operation 17 miles southeast of Phu Bai, Vietnam. Initially a World War II bomber squadron, HMH-463, Marine Aircraft Group 16 (Reinforced), 3rd Marine Aircraft Wing, flew the first CH-53s in Vietnam with the main mission of providing assault support transport, which they still do today. *(DoD Photo National Archive)*

While its initial roots are clearly in the Stoner designs of the early 1950s, like most designs, the multiple lug bolt head, lockup into a barrel extension, and gas system principle can be traced back farther. It was at ArmaLite where this all came together. The first heavy public exposure to the black rifle started in the wet and humid environment of the tropics with the earliest variations sent to US troops in Viet Nam. There were many positive responses at first, but after the ammunition/propellant change, the black rifles were plagued with an extremely lackluster initial impression and poor performance in the field. Problems were eventually minimized after several rounds of intense testing combined with numerous committee change recommendations. Many alterations in production were initiated including chamber dimensions, rifling twist ratios, firing-pin changes, redesigning the flash hider and charging handle, and (against the advice of many people) the addition of a forward assist assembly. Along with ammo and gunpowder refinement, proper maintenance, and problems addressed with early magazines, the early version of black rifle as we know it today was on its way to becoming the cornerstone of the modern American military arsenal.

November 10, 1978. Members of the Norton Air Force Base combat control team hold their Colt Commando assault rifles out of the water as they swim to shore during an amphibious training mission at Lake Isabella, CA. *(DoD photo by SSGT Joseph F. Smith, Jr.)*

As early as 1963, Colt started manufacturing this "new" rifle in semiautomatic only with the civilian population and the law enforcement community in mind. Sold as the AR-15 Sporter it was virtually identical to the M16 with the exception of the fire control group. With an early retail price of $189.50 it was marketed to the hunting and sporting community as a beacon of a new wave of manufacturing technology allowing it to be lightweight while remaining accurate and effective.

Although several minor changes have been made to separate the function of the semiautomatic version of these rifles from their fully automatic relatives over the years, and to keep them from being easily converted to fully automatic, they remain wildly popular and an enormous civilian market thrives today. Numerous upgrades and model enhancements of the civilian line of semiautomatic variants have followed very closely to those designed for the fully automatic models keeping them on a fairly level playing field.

With the 1977 expiration of Gene Stoner's patent on the M16 gas system, several companies sprang up and started manufacturing their own versions of this popular rifle. The trademark model name of "AR-15" was, and still is, owned by Colt, and they are still one of many businesses that manufacture this weapon system and its many configurations.

March 20, 1998. A US Navy SEAL, from SEAL Team 8, holds a Colt 5.56mm M4 Carbine, with a M203 Grenaade Launcher attached, on a firing range in Kuwait as part of the Southwest Asia buildup. *(DoD photo by J02 Charles Neff, USN)*

Modularity is King

At the heart of the black rifle is the versatile lower receiver. This portion of the firearm is the section considered by federal law to be "the firearm" by definition. The lower receiver is the portion of the firearm that contains the trigger group and the pistol grip as well as the magazine well. Also attached to the lower receiver is the buffer tube and stock. This is the part that requires purchase through a licensed federal firearms licensee (if ordered from an out-of-state dealer) and the paperwork that goes along with any other firearm purchase, depending upon the

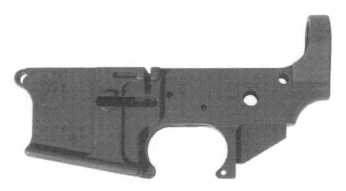

This is the "heart" of the entire black rifle system, the lower receiver This particular lower receiver was manufactured by Sun Devil Manufacturing of Mesa, AZ.

laws of the State of the buyer. Every other part of this firearm may be ordered directly by the end user and requires no federal licensing or paperwork. All other parts, including the upper receivers and the barrels are treated just like any other non-regulated parts.

The upper receiver plays an equally important role in the mechanism. The upper receiver is the point of attachment for the barrel and the housing for the bolt, bolt carrier and charging handle. It is attached to the lower receiver by two takedown pins that are operable without the aid of any tools. The upper and lower receivers may be separated and rejoined at any time without fear of losing any components under normal handling. This may be attractive for size considerations when breaking down for transportation or when changing the characteristics of the rifle for a specific task.

This is the upper receiver. Upper receivers, once barreled, can be easily swapped around on different lower receivers to create new configurations for specific applications.

Several rifle configurations may be assembled on a single lower receiver simply by swapping out barreled upper receivers. Specific tasks may require features unique to that task but may not be desirable to others. This is where the real beauty of the black rifle comes in. Unlike most other firearms, the characteristics of the black rifle can be altered at any time, and reversed back again, just by changing upper receivers. It is indeed more than a weapon; it is truly a "weapon system" as it is often properly referred as.

This is one lower receiver and 3 different upper receivers that can be moved on or off the lower receiver to meet different needs.

For obvious reasons, an entry-type rifle may consist of a very short barrel and either iron sights or a zero-magnification dot-type sight. A varmint hunting rifle may be much more effective with a long barrel and high power telescopic sight. With a black rifle, both of these configurations are only a quick upper receiver swap away with no lack of performance in either field.

There are barrels ranging from the 7-inch* "Kitty Kat" barrel from DPMS (www.dpmsinc.com) to a 24-inch Varminter Extra Heavy Barrel from Bushmaster Firearms (www.bushmaster.com) and a multitude of lengths in between. (* Under Federal Law a rifle barrel has to be over 16 inches in length to be a legal Title I firearm. By purchasing or registering the rifle as a Short Barreled Rifle, the owner can use any barrel length at will. With registered machine guns, the barrel length is not a legal stipulation under Federal Law and any length barrel may be used). There are not many rifles that allow the flexibility of swapping out barrel lengths without the necessity of tools in less than 30 seconds like this system. Additionally, another major advantage is the sights are part of the upper receiver as well, so there is no need to re-zero after making this swap. If multiple barreled upper receivers are owned, they can all be sighted-in and swapped as desired with a complete return to zero with careful handling and the correct ammunition.

From Plinking to Protecting

If there is any one thing that can always be counted on in the firearms community, it is American ingenuity and the desire to make something bigger and better. (Sometimes smaller is better, in this case.) Fortunately, this has proven to work well in transforming the once light .223 Rem. (5.56x45mm) rifle into something left only to one's imagination and budget. With the ease of changing upper receivers, the transformation from the original caliber to a completely new round is almost as simple. Since the upper receiver holds the barrel, bolt and bolt carrier, this is the portion of the rifle where the caliber of the ammunition to be utilized is determined. Thanks to many able minded firearm enthusiasts, these rifles can be converted to almost any caliber ranging from .17 to .50 BMG with minimal (if any) temporary modifications to the lower receiver. From the luxury of plinking for recreation on a budget or additional training, to having the stopping power to assist our front line fighters in the War on Terror, the black rifle can be custom configured to suit every application.

One of the most popular subcaliber units among black rifle shooters is the "Atchisson" .22LR conversion manufactured by Jonathan Arthur Ciener, Inc. (www.22lrconversions.com). When utilized with the recommended ammunition, properly maintained and operated, they provide hours of plinking fun in semiautomatic AR-15s or full automatic fun when used in conjunction with a registered M16. On the opposite end of the ammunition spectrum is the .50BMG Upper Receiver from Watson's Weapons Inc. (www.watsonsweapons.com). This upper receiver actually allows the use of the massive .50 BMG round when attached to your lower receiver. It functions as a single-shot rifle that must be partially taken down to be reloaded between shots.

One of the most popular pistol caliber conversions would include the 9x19mm (Luger) conversion. First introduced in 1985, Colt offered a 9mm blowback-operated submachine gun that worked quite well. Most of the characteristics were the same as the standard rifle, making operation simple for anyone who had utilized or trained on the 5.56x45mm rifle. A special magazine (both 20-round and 32-round) was developed for the much shorter 9x19mm round and a block was pinned inside the standard lower receiver's magazine well to accommodate the smaller magazine while utilizing the same magazine release. A civilian version was soon to follow in semiautomatic only with a 16-inch barrel. Other than the upper receiver and bolt differences, only the buffer was changed to a heavier one, and a few of the trigger group parts were slightly modified. In the 1990s, the US Drug Enforcement Agency adopted a silenced version of this rifle. The Department of Energy also adopted a very short variation known as the Model 633, commonly called a "DoE Upper." The 633 had a 7-inch barrel, collapsible stock and a front handguard to keep the operators hands from straying in front of the muzzle.

Several other companies started manufacturing these pistol caliber conversions with numerous types of feeding systems. While a few emulated the Colt style mag-well block and use the factory Colt 9mm magazines, others used highly modified magazines reworked to fit the interior portion of the factory magazine well. Although many of the modified magazines work very well, they are often expensive and the availability is less than desirable in most cases. Even though there are several manufacturers of aftermarket (any non-Colt) black rifles including several Caliber conversions, the pistol caliber most often encountered remains the 9x19mm.

Feed Me, Seymour!

Like the hungry man-eating plant named Seymour in the 1960s cult classic film Little Shop of Horrors, a black rifle is always hungry and never seems to be fed enough. Firearms, especially those in a military role, are no exception. The earliest magazine design of the AR-15 was a 25-round magazine, which had problems due to being straight, and was immediately replaced with a 20-round magazine. The first ones were steel "waffle" pattern magazines, which were also immediately replaced with the standard aluminum 20-round magazine that eventually evolved into the 20-rounder so common today. In the mid-1960s, a 30-round magazine was manufactured with a slight curve and it seemed to work great in all new rifles but had a hard time feeding in some, including the earlier ones. This was corrected in part by keeping the top portion of the magazine straight like the 20-round version and starting the curvature at the bottom of the magazine well. These magazines still had a reputation for jamming if they were loaded to 30 rounds, and the SOP was load to 28 rounds. This was corrected later by stabilizing the follower with equal leg lengths.

In order to address this "need for feed," Colt experimented with a belt-feed mechanism that operated with a modified upper and lower. With a 20-inch barrel this unit weighed in at almost 8 1/2 pounds without the bipod or ammo box. The belt fed M16 never made it to production.

Fast forward to the early 1980s and bring Jonathan Arthur Ciener back into the picture. A manufacturer primarily specializing in sound suppressors at the time, Jonathan took it upon himself to redesign and reintroduce the concept of a belt-fed AR-15 and M16 and made them available to the general public. When they were evaluated for the now defunct Machine Gun News in 1992, this writer had the pleasure of working on the article and spending some trigger time with these guns. We were provided with both a semiautomatic model and a fully automatic model. They were built on factory Colt AR-15 and M16 rifles, and like Colts early design the upper and lower receivers were both modified. The Ciener system had a few very interesting points. First, the belt-feed mechanism could be removed from the weapon and it would again accept factory magazines. Second, Ciener produced some of the belt boxes which locked into the magazine well, as in the original design.

We tested them under several conditions with many types of ammunition in semiautomatic and full automatic. We tested it in belt-feed and magazine feed. We tested it with and without the addition of a sound suppressor. In summary it performed excellently. The only drawback was that in the case of a jam it was a "4-handed" operation to clear it and have it up and running quickly, but with a little practice it could be done quite efficiently. It also used a proprietary, modified link that was quite expensive at the time compared to standard unmodified links. These were sold for a few years but were eventually discontinued due to the enormous amount of time necessary to manufacture them.

There are a few current belt-feed systems for the black rifle but nothing yet has reached a mass marketing level. In the March 2003 issue of Small Arms Review (Vol. 6, No. 6), the Shrike 5.56 from Ares Defense (www.aresdefense.com) was covered in great detail as it was due to be released en masse around the time of publication. To this date, it is still being manufactured, released and shipped in very small quantities due to several redesign upgrades and improvements. The great attraction to the Shrike 5.56 is the fact that it works in conjunction with a completely unmodified lower receiver. All attempts at a belt-fed black rifle in the past have required major lower receiver modifications. Like the Ciener, model it can be fired from belt or box magazine but in the case of the Shrike 5.56, when the belt is out, a box magazine is simply inserted, the rifle charged and firing is uninterrupted. There are no parts to take out or change over. We are anxiously awaiting mass shipments of the Shrike 5.56 and will certainly test the newest production model as soon as they are shipped.

Another interesting belt feed option for the black rifle is the XMG from BRP Guns (www.brpguns.com). The XMG34 is essentially an MG34 "upper receiver" designed for use on an M16 lower receiver. Currently in its 5th year of production this inexpensive alternative to an original MG34 has been receiving great reviews for years. Available in 8mm and in .308, they are popping up at ranges nationwide and are becoming more popular with every passing year. They will function in fully automatic when used in conjunction with a registered lower receiver and require only a small (nonpermanent) modification to function. As of this writing, the ATF has reclassified these as firearms and has ruled attachment on a full auto lower to be illegal.

Seeing a need for a belt-fed black rifle that is inexpensive to feed, the master of the miniatures, Lakeside Machine of Tippmann Arms fame decided to design a .22LR belt fed upper receiver with a similar mechanism to the popular Tippmann 1/2 scale miniature machine guns. (www.lakesideguns.com). This upper receiver, available for both semiautomatic and fully automatic function, was tested in the April 2006 (Vol. 9, No. 7) issue of Small Arms Review. The only modifications required to the lower receiver in this assembly are the exchange of the factory buffer and the suggested replacement of the hammer spring.

Here is an example of how far this system has come from its roots. An M16 that is not only belt-fed, but chambered in .22 Long Rifle. This conversion is just a replacement upper receiver with the addition of a special drop-in buffer system.

Understanding the demand for more ammo capacity than the 30-round magazines were able to provide, the Beta Company, of Atlanta, Georgia (www.betaco.com) worked with Jim Sullivan of the old

ArmaLite and the M16 design fame, the original inventor of the 100-round C-Mag. Sullivan worked as a consultant with Beta Company in the early developmental stages of the new Beta C-Mag and with the introduction and advances in plastic materials and its ability to keep tight tolerances the C-MAG as we know it today has developed into an extremely reliable system, all while keeping weight to a minimum.

The 100-round .223 Beta C-Mag. Proper maintenance requires the use of dry lubrication.

Mounting Madness

We live in a market driven economy and combined with the simple truth that necessity is the mother of invention, some "solutions" have been presented to us for "problems" we may never have known existed otherwise. In the last several years there have been an enormous number of accessories manufactured for mounting on MIL-STD-1913 rails. Along with these accessories came a mad rush for mounting platforms, and the standard factory handguards on the AR-15 and M16 are quickly being antiquated and replaced with new and improved rail systems. There are several to choose from including the Knight Rail Interface System (RIS) and Rail Adapter System (RAS) (www.knightarmco.com), VLTOR VIS System (www.vltor.com), POF-USA Predator Rail System (www.pof-usa.com), LMT Monolithic Rail Platform (www.lewismachine.net) and many more. All of the aforementioned have been of excellent quality.

For those not needing the precision, or wishing to spend the amount of money those mentioned may cost, some simple handguard replacements have been introduced that incorporate rails into them and some rail adaptors have been manufactured that simply bolt on to the existing A2-type handguards. A few of those have been utilized for testing devices like vertical grips where a slight amount of movement was not detrimental to the system and they performed fine. Other applications like mounting optics or more "load bearing" accessories would probably not be recommended for the latter systems.

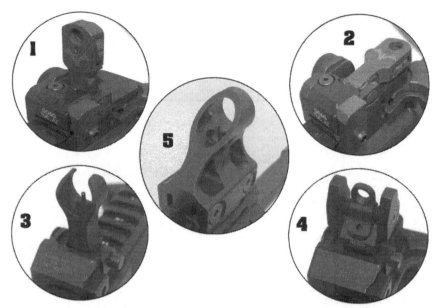

A few of the many rail mounted BUIS (Back Up Iron Sights) available today. 1 – GG&G rear site made for DoubleSTar in the "up" position. 2 – GG&G rear site made for DoubleStar in the "down" position. 3 – Troy Industries front folding battle sight in the "up" position. 4 – Troy Industries rear folding battle sight in the "up" position. 5 – POF-USA FTA2005 Front Sight. It does not fold but has a unique "hooded" design making target acquisition fast and accurate while remaining very strong.

All the new configurations and types of intended deployments these systems are capable of bring the necessity of new support equipment. One area where a serious advancement has been made is in the sighting systems available. Electronic "dot type" sights are very popular for close-up work and there are many types and styles. A few extremely popular systems include the EOTech Holographic Sight (www.eotech-inc.com), the Aimpoint CompM4 (www.aimpoint.com) and the Trijicon ACOG (www.trijicon.com). While each system has distinct advantages the author is very familiar with the EOTech model 552. It has several settings for use with a night vision monocular as well as the standard day settings. The Holographic Sight is placed in a forward position on the top rail and utilized as usual during normal daylight. During low light the monocular is mounted behind it so the operator can use it at night without having to re-zero the weapon.

Along with the popularity of low or zero magnification electronic sights, the demand for a well-made, high quality, Back Up Iron Sight (BUIS) has been high for use during a potential electronic failure. Several contenders on the market include the Troy Industries, Inc. Folding Battle Sight (www.troyind.com), the GG&G Flip-Up Sights (www.gggaz.com), and A.R.M.S. Inc., #40 Folding Sights (www.armsmounts.com). An interesting front sight is the POF-USA FTA2005 Front Sight. It is not a folding sight but a stationary sight that is hooded for an extremely fast target acquisition and has been found to be complementary to use in conjunction with "dot-type" sights or as a standalone with the correct rear BUIS. Due to the great number of new sight requirements, many of the modern rifles are available with a removable carry handle. Once the familiar carry handle and rear sight is removed, a standard MIL-STD-1913 rail is exposed to be used alone or in conjunction with these new sights and rail systems.

Another interesting new front sight was recently introduced for the black rifle. It is made by KNS Precision (www.knsprecisioninc.com) and is actually a circular "peep" with a crosshair in it. Initial testing appears it is fast and accurate and we are anxious to spend more time with this new front sight as well as several more of their latest offerings.

As a Catch-22, these new mounting platforms that were spawned from new items in need of mounts have spun off their own items made to be mounted on this newly available space. There are several devices available for mounting on MIL-STD-1913 rails including visible lasers, IR lasers, and lights. optics, night vision, camera equipment and many more items. Some earlier available items that were designed to mount on standard handguards or directly on the barrel have even been redesigned to mount directly on a rail system due to the high proliferation on later models. A prime example is the new rail mount 40mm LMT M203 Grenade Launcher. This tried and true M16 accessory used to mount on the barrel of the standard black rifle and a special handguard replaced the factory A1 or A2 handguard issued with the rifle. With the new rail mounted version, no additional handguards are necessary and due to the nature of the mounting system there is no longer any stress on the barrel as it is allowed to free-float with many current rail systems.

AR Accessories

As mentioned previously, several companies exist today just to service this weapon system. A quick glance around the Internet or any large, stocking gun shop will uncover thousands of items geared toward users of the AR-15 and M16 weapon systems. A look at KNS Precision and their product line will unveil several components for the black rifle useful in simple preservation roles such as pins that are designed not to rotate and egg-hole the aluminum receivers at the thin section supporting the hammer and trigger pins. They carry a variety of sights for target, plinking, competition and tactical applications and even manufacture a set of Spade Grips so you can shoot the rifle in the same manner as a 1919A4 with butterfly grips or an M60D model. We tested these grips in the May 2007 (Vol. 10, No. 8) issue of Small Arms Review and we found them a blast to shoot, especially with a pintle mount and Beta C-MAG. They are well made and functioned flawlessly.

While you are in research mode, take a peek at some of the products in the Command Arms Accessories line (www.commandarms.com). Some of these accessories manufactured for the AR-15 and M16 weapon system look more like they came back from a fact finding mission from the 22nd Century than from Ivyland, Pennsylvania where they are located. With accessories and upgrades from butt-stock to muzzle, the only part of the original weapon system that looks familiar is the distinct shape of the receiver section. Watch for a piece in an upcoming issue of Small Arms Review where we take a "Plain Jane" AR-15 and give it the complete CAA treatment while testing it every step of the way. We are looking for something that really enhances performance and not just cosmetics and we have been assured we will not be disappointed.

Back to the Future

There is one unique feature of the black rifle that is as controversial as all other designs combined. This would be the way the gas system of the firearm operates and whether changing it is considered an upgrade or downgrade by the user. The black rifle operates with a direct impingement gas system in the following manner. When the rifle is fired, the rotating bolt is in its locked position in the barrel extension. As the bullet passes a gas port located under the front sight, some gas is bled off into a gas port and directed through a gas tube to the rear. The hot gas pressurizes the gas tube and the rear end of the pressurized tube is the gas key located on top of the bolt carrier with the gas thus exerting rearward pressure on this movable part. This pressure starts the bolt carrier traveling rearward, unlocking the bolt via its cam pin in the cam path on the carrier, and initiating the extraction. The bolt carrier travels rearward, and the projectile exits the bore evacuating the pressurized gas from the gas tube, ending any rearward pressure from the gas system. That time under pressure is critical to reliability and is dictated by the amount of time the bullet is traveling in front of the gas port. As the bolt carrier passes into the buffer tube (concealed in the stock) the fired casing is ejected. Met with a forward amount of spring tension from the now compressed buffer spring, the bolt carrier is returned to the front, picking up a new round from the magazine, loading it in the chamber and rotating and locking the bolt to restart the sequence.

The problems with this particular system are multiple. It is dumping combustion byproduct - "dirt" - into the same place it feeds ammunition from. This leaves a lot of carbon buildup over time and can create function problems when not maintained regularly. The lower receiver and its trigger group are often heavily soiled from this gas system and it is compounded numerous times over when combined with the use of a sound suppressor. Due to the carbon, unburned powder and extra heat following the path of least resistance, the extra back pressure created with the use of a silencer leaves more debris than normal and blowback is often an unpleasant effect inflicted on the shooter. On top of the maintenance issue, which in the recreational shooting world should be a no-brainer, is an issue not often spoken about. As indicated before, the additional debris is carried back into the action of the gun and it is carried by very hot gas. It has been suggested by some people that the effect of these hot gasses under heavier than normal shooting conditions could cause metal temperament problems over time. A heavy influx of heating and cooling could create some structural problems with extremely heavy use.

There are several systems that now use a gas piston system in place of the direct impingement system and Small Arms Review has covered several of them in the past. In the last two years we have examined the HK416 System, the POF P-416 System and just recently, the Colt LE1020 Advanced Law Enforcement Carbine. Fairly recently, Ares Defense introduced their GSR-35 Black Lightning system, which is a drop-in piston kit that takes the place of the original gas tube and bolt carrier. Leitner-Wise Rifle Company (www.lwrifles.com) also specializes in a piston system however we have not had the opportunity to evaluate it yet. While the concept is certainly nothing new, (Colt experimented with a piston system in the 1960s, and there are many other examples pre-dating that) its time certainly seems to have come and it appears to be here to stay.

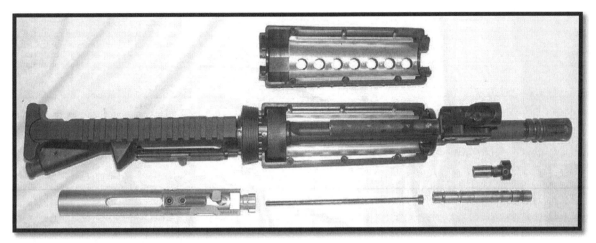

The POF P-416 Gas Piston Upper Receiver field stripped. This system consists of a gas plug, gas piston, op-rod, and a heavily modified bolt carrier.

Other than a brief amount of time spent working with an early "Rhino System" in the early 1990s, of all the systems mentioned above, this writer only has an extensive amount of time on the POF P-416 system at this point. Other SAR contributors have extensive trigger time on the HK416, and will cover other systems in the future. On the POF system that I have tested, there are definite advantages that have been witnessed, primarily the number of rounds it is able to run with little or no maintenance with no malfunctions. The POF P-416 utilizes C.R.O.S. (Corrosion Resistant Operating System) where their major components are impregnated with silicon nickel creating an incredibly slick surface. After firing several thousand rounds, the surface easily wipes clean with only a dry cloth, and after almost 20,000 rounds in one particular test unit there is no visible wear on any of the coated parts.

During initial testing the system was fired in excess of 9,000 rounds with no maintenance or lubrication of any kind and when it was finally cleaned because we thought there was a single failure to feed, ending the endurance test, it was later found that it was a faulty magazine creating the feeding problem and not the gun itself. Another factor that assists the P-416 system in functioning so well under harsh treatment is the fact that there are no gas rings necessary since there is no actual gas pushed back into the bolt carrier. This seems to translate into a firearm that will operate in a harsher environment due to much lighter tolerances. Without the presence of gas rings creating a seal between the bolt and bolt carrier, everything moves much smoother and is less meticulous in its typically tight tolerances.

If there is an immediately noticeable advantage in this particular gas piston system it is durability. On top of the several thousand rounds fired with no maintenance except for the initial cleaning after the perceived stoppage, many of them have been in a succession so rapid that it would have been certain failure for a direct impingement system; melting the gas tube and ending the testing very early on. After years of testing black rifles, the author has a collection of failed gas tubes, many resembling spaghetti found lying on top of the barrel after reaching the point of failure. If there are any immediate disadvantages of this gas piston system over a direct impingement system, this author has not yet noticed them.

Now Left Can Be Right

A fantastic example of how the civilian market often takes its own direction and even has the potential to influence the military marketplace is a manufacturer from New Britain Connecticut named Stag Arms, LLC. (www.stagarms.com). Founded in May of 2003, Stag decided to cater to a percentage of the market who had been all but ignored for years. They completely redesigned the upper receiver, bolt and bolt carrier to eject from the left, specifically for left-handed shooters. Featured in the March 2006 (Vol. 9, No. 6) issue of Small Arms Review, southpaws will never again have to depend on a brass deflector keeping hot brass from hitting them or crossing their line of fire.

The Future

It is the versatility of the AR-15/M16 that has allowed it to adapt and thrive in so many differing environments and it is the modularity of the system that is a direct contributor to its survival and evolution. There are a few companies that are addressing this in ways that could never have been originally conceived 40 years ago and will lead the way into a long future for the black rifle.

MGI (www.mgimilitary.com) has been in the black rifle business for decades. Their upgrades have been chronicled in the pages of Small Arms Review several times including their Rate Reducing Buffer - May 2004 (Vol. 7, No. 8), The QCB Upper Receiver - December 2004 (Vol. 8, No. 3) and most recently The Hydra Modular Weapon System - May 2007 (Vol. 10, No. 8). With such versatility as a quick-change barrel upper receiver that requires no tools and works with original factory barrels, changes in length, style and caliber have never been faster, easier or less expensive. The Marck-15 Lower Receiver with interchangeable magazine wells, again with no tools, allows the correct magazine to be used to coincide with the caliber being fired. For example, if you are utilizing a 7.62x37 barrel and bolt, you can use the AK mag-well and utilize standard AK47 magazines. This ensures the correct feed and presentation rather than redesigning a new magazine around an existing space and angle. Mags are inexpensive, available and reliable. Next in the works is a 9mm SMG mag-well that will utilize the factory Colt 9mm SMG magazines. Several new offerings are in the pipeline, some certain to be out even before this magazine hits the newsstand.

Cobb Manufacturing (www.cobb50.com) has a line of rifles called the MCR (Multi Caliber Rifle) and it is based on the design characteristics of the AR-15, just a little bigger. The MCR is a semiautomatic, gas operated system that can be chambered in a long list of calibers from 9mm to 338 Lapua, designed originally for the SCAR rifle program. They are far from newcomers to the industry and have been dealing with such innovative firearms as the .50 BMG FA50 and BA50 for several years. Teamed up with top-line suppressor manufacturers their systems are well made and versatile.

With the "feeding" frenzy a constant issue as discussed previously, we expect to see upgrades and alterations to this portion of the weapon system as long as it is in use. Just before finishing this article the author received what is perhaps the latest offering to the high-capacity quest to evaluate for a future article. It is the CL-Mag from Armatac Industries, Inc. (www.armatac.com). Resembling the Beta C-MAG in shape, the CL-Mag is manufactured from aircraft aluminum and holds 150 rounds of 5.56x45mm. Finished in a hard coat type III anodized finish, it is intended to work in all AR-15/M16 variants. We are anxious to proceed with testing this new feeding system in the near future.

Conclusion

Since there is really nothing to compare the popularity of this unique weapon system to, with its longevity in both military and civilian applications, it is the opinion of this writer that the sheer ability to act as a chameleon and adapt to almost every environment is the life force behind its ever growing popularity. It has to be noted that many of the upgrades and enhancements are civilian based ideas with no military spec sheet giving them direction. Some of these ideas and items can be looked at as simply "fun" and that is an important aspect of shooting that some of us who are a little too hung up on being "professionals" tend to overlook a little too often. Not everything that is discovered or tested has to have an adrenaline soaked special operations application in mind. Some of the best gear for our professional applications stands a chance of starting out as a light-hearted civilian product, just because it is looked at and designed with fresh, new, untainted eyes. Some of the greatest design innovations this writer has witnessed have come from challenges from people who specifically stated that in their professional opinion something couldn't be done.

With an ever-changing requirement for the ultimate weapon system in this unpredictable War on Terror, if any weapon stands the test of time it is the AR-15/M16. With a virtual flood of new accessories, upgrades, calibers, finishes, furniture and design enhancements being introduced at breakneck speed, this writer has a hard time even thinking of the day where the black rifle or some form of it is not going to be the basis for our primary service weapon for at least 40 more years.

Author's Note: While this article started out to be a short overview of the AR-15/M16 and its longevity, it soon became obvious that it could not be done in just a few words. The system is too complex and the changes, alterations and upgrades are far too numerous to simply skim over and condense. Unfortunately, due to space constraints, it had to end somewhere and we were not able to include every single company that offers firearms and accessories related to this weapon system. They are far too numerous, and even a quick glance through the pages of Small Arms Review will reveal several more businesses who specialize in parts and accessories for the black rifle. It is not our intention to promote anyone in particular while leaving anyone else out, nor should either be misconstrued as an endorsement or lack of such in the latter case. We would be happy to put together a condensed Black Rifle Buyers Guide listing every business related to this system in the future, but had no room to so in this article.

The AR-15: The Ultimate Modular Rifle

It can be argued that there is no rifle as versatile as the AR-15. There are an unlimited number of configurations possible, and an amazing number of caliber conversions, with more joining the ranks every day. One of the best features of this rifle system is that you can have almost every possible combination without ever having to buy another rifle. For the budget minded gun collector or for the person who just eventually gets bored with every gun over time and needs a new fix, the AR-15 is your dream gun come true. The mere purchase of one rifle, some basic tools and a small budget for "extra parts" now and then can keep your gun collection looking fresh.

The lower receiver is the part of this rifle that is considered by the Bureau of Alcohol, Tobacco and Firearms to be "the firearm". This is the part the pistol grip is connected to and carries all the model information and serial numbers. In order to purchase the lower receiver, whether it is part of a complete rifle or as a stand-alone item you must fill out an ATF form 4473 (yellow sheet). If you wish to purchase a lower receiver from an out of state source you must go through a licensed gun dealer.

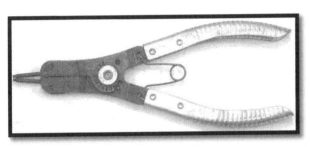

Inside and outside snap ring pliers are a necessity for removing or replacing the retaining ring when changing barrels on an upper receiver.

Every other part of the AR-15 can be purchased direct from dealers, distributors and manufacturers with no local dealer required. The other parts are not regulated. This being the case, that one lower receiver can be transformed into almost any configuration with a simple phone call to one of the several AR-15 parts dealers in this very publication. These new parts can be delivered directly to your home and assembled into your "new" rifle at your convenience.

After you flip through these pages and decide what you want your "new" rifle to look like, you are going to need to find a local RKI in the AR-15 field. (Reasonably Knowledgeable Individual is a phrase coined by Dan Shea back in the old days of Machine Gun News Magazine and makes reference to someone with an above average knowledge in their particular field without having to wear the "Expert" title or to carry any of the excess baggage that comes with that title.) It would also be wise to purchase some of the many books written about the AR-15.

Your next mission will be to obtain the tools necessary to disassemble your rifle from its current configuration and to install the new parts. Your configuration change can be very simple, as in changing only the furniture to go from the early SP1 look to the newer A2 style and this would require far less tools than swapping barrels on your existing upper receiver. You don't need to purchase every gunsmithing tool in one shot but you should look into the correct tools necessary each time you modify your gun.

If you are going to just swap furniture, all you really need may be a screwdriver, an allen wrench and a good strong handgrip. If you are going to buy a new upper receiver and leave the original lower receiver alone, you may not need any tools at all. If you are going to change out your trigger group to a newer 2-stage trigger, or add a new double wall gas tube, or re-barrel your original upper you will need a good set of punches, barrel blocks, special wrenches and lots of patience at first. If you are going to purchase a stripped lower receiver and assemble it from scratch to get started, you are going to need even more specialty tools to complete the assembly.

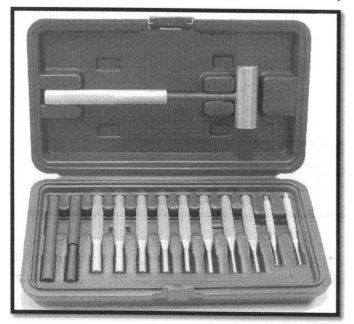

A good punch set is a necessity for working on firearms.

Everyone skimps a little on the correct tools at first but it is important to remember that you are working on a firearm here with a fair value. The correct tools will allow you to work on it with a minimal amount of problems and that translates into fewer scratches and other "whoop's". Having the correct tools also make the project much easier to complete. These tools are readily available from the advertisers in these pages and most of the regular AR-15 parts suppliers carry a full line of these specialty tools in inventory. They can also assist you in learning what tools you may need for each application.

When you are changing the configuration of your rifle it is important to remember that just because almost any part will interchange between guns, the final product may not be legal without prior registration with BATF, or it may not be legal at all. If you start out with a pre-ban "assault rifle" you can avoid many legal hassles associated with "manufacturing a post-ban assault rifle". Just having the pre-ban rifle to start with allows you to purchase barrels with bayonet lugs and flash hiders. If you start with a post-ban rifle, it must remain in a post-ban configuration such as no collapsing stock, bayonet lug or flash hider. Most of the parts suppliers now carry almost identical parts kits that will fit either category to keep you on the right side of the law. Just make sure that you mention to the supplier which rifle you are starting with.

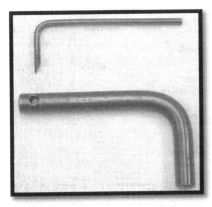

These tools are worth their weight in gold for installing the front push pin retaining pin and spring in the lower receiver. The author has launched several of these tiny pins into space trying to complete the installation without these tools.

Another configuration problem you should be aware of is maintaining the correct legal barrel length. If you are starting with a 20" barreled, full size pre-ban rifle, you can buy a carbine parts kit and install a 16" barrel and collapsible stock but the barrel cannot be shorter than 16". Almost every parts dealer sells barrels and barreled upper receivers as short as 10", and yes they would look pretty darn sexy on your new carbine, but this would change the status of your firearm to an illegal short barreled rifle. These short uppers are sold primarily as machine gun replacement barrels where barrel length is not an issue. Should you wish to install one of these on your semi-auto, pre-ban rifle you may do so, but you need to fill out a BATF Form 1 (see Small Arms Review Vol. 1 No. 10) and have it approved prior to ordering the short barrel. Without doing so the mere possession of the short barrel combined with possession of a semi lower receiver can constitute possession of an unregistered short barreled rifle.

You also want to be aware of the differences between some problematic M16 parts that can be interchange with your AR-15 parts and also cause legal problems. Just as serious as the barrel length, the mere possession of an M16 trigger, sear, bolt carrier, hammer or disconnector combined with possession of a semi auto AR-15 lower can constitute possession of an unregistered machine gun. You don't want to go there. Make sure you specify to the parts dealer that you are building a SEMI and again, whether it is a POST BAN rifle or a PRE BAN rifle.

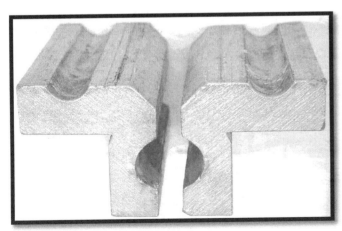

You will need a set of barrel blocks for your vice to re-barrel an upper receiver.

The photos placed on the pages with this book represent just a small sampling of the many configurations possible to have with the same lower receiver. These photos were taken on a few different ones. (Please refer to the last sentence). Some of the handguards or flash hiders don't necessarily match the correct upper receiver's to emulate originals, but you can build any combination you wish. The sky is the limit. Of course, there is no guarantee that you won't like all the configurations and you even many want to own them all at once. This means several lower receivers and much more expense but, hey, who is sweating the details.

Birth of a Black Rifle -
From Barstock to Bushmaster

Exclusive Industry Profile

In some parts of the world the word "Bushmaster" will conjure up images of large, venomous snakes. A member of the pit viper family, it is known for its lethality and is found in Central and South America. In circles of firearms enthusiasts and for members of the military and law enforcement, the same word is synonymous with quality AR-15 and M16 type rifles that are manufactured in the northern most state in New England.

For the first time in history, Bushmaster Firearms of Windham, Maine has allowed outside photographic equipment into their facilities. Small Arms Review was invited to visit Bushmaster Firearms to chronicle portions of the manufacturing process of their famous version of the Black Rifle.

Company History

Originally incorporated in 1973, Bushmaster Firearms concentrated their manufacturing efforts on the Bushmaster Arm Pistol, a survival gun designed for pilots during the Vietnam War. The Arm Pistol, along with a companion rifle known as the Bushmaster Assault Rifle utilized some parts from the M16 rifle family while employing an op-rod system similar to that used by the Soviet AK-47.

Following a company reorganization in 1980, Bushmaster Firearms, Inc. started to focus their efforts in selling AR-15 and M16 parts and eventually began to manufacture their own line of AR-15 and M16 replacement parts for sale. In 1983, the first complete rifles bearing the Bushmaster name were manufactured in Portland, Maine. Five years later the company relocated to their current location in

Windham, Maine. Bushmaster Firearms, Inc. now owns a 52,000 square foot facility at their 19 acre business park and employs over 80 people at this location.

In 2002, Bushmaster established their Western Division in Lake Havasu City, Arizona. This division of Bushmaster Firearms, Inc. is dedicated to manufacturing a Carbon Fiber series of the AR-15 and M16 type firearms. This Western division now has over 25 full time employees and occupies 12,000 square feet to house their state of the art injection molding and CNC equipment.

Quality First

With so many companies currently competing in the AR-15 and M16 market, our first question was an obvious one; "What makes Bushmaster stand out in such a large market?" Their answer came as fast as the question was asked and was simple enough: "Q-U-A-L-I-T-Y." Even though they have an extremely diverse product line of quality products, the general feeling at Bushmaster is that their quality control is their best selling point. When we asked for an example, we were directed to their Quality Control (QC) building and allowed to sit in as their barrels underwent their normal series of tests.

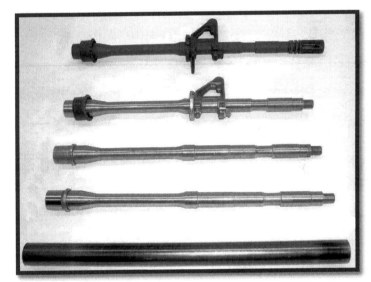

The barrel manufacturing process involves several steps. From bottom to top: the stock material is drilled, button rifled and stress relieved; it is then turned and head spaced; the barrel is chrome lined next; the gas port is drilled and the front sight is indexed; after passing quality control checks between each stage, the barrel is finally phosphate finished.

Bushmaster barrels are manufactured from Chrome-Moly Vanadium Steel or from 416 Match Grade Stainless Steel. Each process of manufacturing has to undergo numerous levels of testing in order to progress to the next stage of manufacturing. The barrel stock material is first drilled, button rifled and stress relieved. After undergoing a series of QC tests, all barrels that pass are turned to their intended profile and head spaced. Following another round of QC testing the barrels are chrome lined and tested again. All barrels that pass this stage go on to have the gas ports drilled and front sights indexed followed by a phosphate finishing.

In between each of these steps, the barrels are bore scoped and air gauged. When a barrel is bore scoped a technician runs an extremely powerful microscope all the way down the inside of the barrel. An image is projected onto a monitor and the technician actually visually inspects the inside of the barrel looking for flaws or abnormalities. In the process of testing the barrels with an air gauge, the barrels are pressurized and an indicator rod is slowly run through the length of the barrel watching for a drop or increase in pressure, indicating either a tight area or loose area not visible to the eye even while bore scoping. Any deviation outside of Bushmasters strict specifications will cause the barrel to "fail" and it will never see the next step in the manufacturing process.

To go a step further, even though the barrels undergo Magnetic Particle Testing they are also checked utilizing an Eddy Current. Magnetic Particle Testing is a process fairly common to AR-15 and M16 Barrel manufacturing and most people may have noticed the "passing marks" on their barrels in the past. The familiar "CMP" mark often seen would indicate Colt Magnetic Particle Testing and "BMP" would indicate Bushmaster Magnetic Particle Testing and so on. Magnetic Particle Testing is a process that checks the integrity of ferromagnetic parts by looking for microscopic cracks. During this testing, when a

Initial forgings of Bushmaster upper and lower receiver assemblies on the left with their machined counterparts to the right. After machining is done they still must pass another stage of inspection before being finished with a baked dry-lube film and hard anodized with a nickel acetate final seal coat.

crack is present, an amount of magnetic flux will gather at that spot attracting magnetic particles allowing the flaw to be discovered. Testing with an Eddy Current goes even farther and allows the operator to electronically "look through" the metal checking for structural integrity, case depth and hardness while also allowing the ability to "see" cracks, pits, seams or otherwise invisible surface flaws. Finally, head spacing is checked on 100% of the Bushmaster barrels rather than just a random sampling.

Bushmaster utilizes a similar quality control regimen on all of their parts including their lower and upper receiver sections as they progress from raw material to the initial forgings to their finished and assembled states.

Once all of the individual parts have passed every step of quality control and final finishing, it is time for their assembly. All firearms assembly is completed in house with each gun going through several "assembly stations." Each station specializes in one specific area of assembly and as the firearms ascend towards completion they end up at the test-firing portion of the facility. Every Bushmaster firearm is laser bore sighted and test fired before being shipped. Every semiautomatic firearm is fired a prescribed number of rounds in rapid succession and every round must feed and fire perfectly in order to pass this final test and go on to inventory for shipping. The test-firing requirement for each full automatic firearm is similar to this, with more rounds fired and the firing is also done in full auto.

Final assembly of the Bushmaster rifle is completed in many different stages utilizing several work stations. Bushmaster employs over 80 people in their Windham, Maine facility and they have several people who specialize in each aspect of manufacture, production, quality control, assembly, and finishing.

A Diverse Product Line

Since the early days of the Arm Pistol, Bushmaster Firearms, Inc. has introduced and currently includes an enormous number of items in their product line, with over 50 different firearms and several hundred parts and accessories available for sale. From the typical AR-15 and M16 style firearms used as the primary service weapon of the United States Armed Services for over 40 years, to the newest Carbon Fiber firearms technology, Bushmaster

Several racks of finished Bushmaster rifles await shipping.

strives to have something for everyone. Their current offerings range in caliber from .22LR variants all the way up to .308 (7.62x51mm NATO) models and range in size from pistol configurations up to their 24-inch heavy barreled varmint series.

The Bushmaster M17S Bullpup Carbine may be one of the most unique firearms in the Bushmaster product line. The M17S affords the shooter a 21.5 inch barrel on a package with an overall length of only 30 inches. It is a short stroke piston, gas operated semiautomatic rifle and is chambered in 5.56x45mm. It utilizes standard AR-15/M16 magazines.

As well as servicing the U.S. commercial firearms market, Bushmaster Firearms, Inc. currently manufactures arms for U.S. law enforcement, governmental agencies and foreign military forces. Short-barreled rifles, law enforcement and post 1986 dealer sample machine guns are all available with prior BATFE (and at times, State Department) approval.

Custom Build Your Own Black Rifle

If the television reality-show craze were to momentarily abort political correctness and expand into the gun world, there could certainly be potential in a new series called Pimp-My-Rifle. Just like the auto industry and the homebuilders have done, a bone-stock firearm could be presented for enhancement and returned to its owner in a highly modified configuration. Unfortunately, for the time being, no such reality show exists but thanks to the folks at CAA, many upgrades from mild to wild can privately be accomplished with a single phone call.

The starting rifle in our build project. A basic rifle with no high-end accessories can be purchased for an amount that most would consider reasonable and can be customized later.

Plastic Rifle Popularity

There are several companies who specialize in manufacturing AR-15 style rifles in configurations too numerous to list here. The popularity of the semiautomatic version of America's primary service weapon has exploded onto the civilian gun scene in the last decade evidenced by the number of major "sporting rifle" manufacturers who have added a version of the Black Rifle to their lineup. A firearm once considered on the fringe, or of limited interest, the AR-15 style rifle is no longer only being produced by specialized companies catering primarily to a military or law enforcement market. Eying a desirable and profitable market share, such well-known manufacturers as Remington, High Standard and Smith & Wesson seem to have now embraced the firearm that companies such as Colt, Bushmaster, DPMS, Olympic Arms, DoubleStar, and so many others have specialized in for decades.

With so many gun owners joining the ranks of the Black Rifle Owners Club, there has been a major influx of new ideas, points of view and weapon objectives brought forth by the fresh customer base and a desire to adapt this platform to their particular shooting discipline. This has, in turn, boosted the accessory market in volume and innovation. Jumping directly into the deep-end of the demand issue, CAA has a huge line of accessories for these rifles that continues to grow at an amazing pace. Their product line creates an environment where someone can purchase a standard, basic rifle and accessorize it for their particular purpose. Unfortunately, there have been specific cases where sensory overload occurred (too many available options and configurations) at a time when a purchase was about to be made and has led to a lost sale because the potential buyer wanted to "buy the right rifle the first time" and needed to do more research before buying.

Overload Problem Solved

One of the greatest advantages of the Black Rifle is the complete modularity built into the system. Almost any configuration in almost any caliber can be obtained with a little assistance from the aftermarket accessory industry. This means that for some shooters, especially those new to the AR-15 style rifle, the initial purchase can be as easy as a stripped-down, basic rifle, and it can be later customized to fit the specific criteria the new owner would desire. As well as making the initial purchase easier, this strategy has the potential to save the end user a substantial amount of money. Best of all, the configuration can be altered again, an unlimited number of times if desired, if a different or ever-changing end use should occur.

The CAA Stock is one of the upgrades that really added to the overall rifle. It is much more comfortable, allows several attachment points for slings and accessories and even incorporates a hidden battery box to hold 4 of the popular CR123 batteries, which so many tactical lights and lasers now use.

From Practical to Tactical... and Beyond

There is always plenty of discussion about what is considered a legitimate and useful accessory versus what constitutes an accessory deemed silly or ineffective. Ultimately this decision has to be the choice of the end user. This statement comes with a few light-hearted warnings.

* Black Rifle Bling - If you find something you can't live without, hanging off the barrel of your Black Rifle, but it is a little "outside the box," the ribbing from your peers is just part of the game. There are several accessories available and only you can decide what will meet your requirements. A light, a foregrip or a laser, are usually acceptable in most shooting social circles. A bayonet lug mounted multi-blade combination lock-pick and hot dog fork might not.

- The 20-pound Light Rifle - Almost universally taunted by veteran AR-15 type rifle owners are those who purchase every accessory to the point of concealing the identity of the original firearm, and are often lightheartedly referred to as "Mall Ninjas" or "Internet Commandos." Some guns have been intentionally over-accessorized and photographed for the web to poke a little fun at these, and some are even quite humorous. You will have to decide what you need for your new rifle based on the purpose you want it for. Just don't mount everything you can find, anywhere it will fit, all at once.

If you are new to these rifles and maybe a little overwhelmed by the number of accessories available, consider these previous points your fair warning. They may save you some seemingly vicious but light-hearted ribbing.

The Right Touch

In order to demonstrate a series of practical upgrades to a base rifle, this writer contacted Command Arms Accessories (CAA) and explained the concept. They were asked to choose some of their popular accessories for a "makeover" on a basic rifle. In a very short period of time a few boxes arrived with sev-

The vertical front grip chosen also doubles as a flashlight adapter. With the button (A) at the rear, the light can be turned on within easy reach of the thumb. By depressing the button on the side (B), it can be changed from an intermittent switch to a standard on/off switch.

eral accessories and with the addition of a few components laying around the workshop, the first magazine version of Pimp-My-Rifle was underway.

The base rifle we started with had a low-end collapsible stock, a flattop upper receiver, standard front carbine-length forend, stock pistol grip and a traditional front sight & gas block.

- Stock - The makeover started at the rear and moved forward towards the muzzle. The first step was to deal with the factory stock. It was replaced with a CAA Collapsible Stock. This new stock gives the shooter a better cheek-weld and includes a no-slip rubber recoil pad as well as a small compartment that holds 4 CR123 Batteries, a short Picatinny accessory rail and an optional push-button sling swivel.

- Sling - With a mounting hole at the front of the new stock available, a one-point sling from CAA was chosen for this application. One-point slings work well in tight quarters and assist in weapon retention while incorporating quick-detach connection points.

- Pistol Grip - The stock pistol grip was replaced with a CAA Ergonomic Grip. This grip is a little wider, incorporates finger grooves and completely fills the space above the grip to the rear of the receiver for a very comfortable hold.

- Sights - Since this rifle had only a flattop receiver and standard front sight post, a combination of dot-type scope and adjustable iron sights were added and co-witnessed. They can be used in combination with each other or used individually if necessary or desired. The rear sight chosen was an LMT Tactical Adjustable Rear Sight. It is completely adjustable for windage and elevation. The red-dot scope chosen was a 30mm S.P.O.T. scope and mount from MGI Military. With several dot intensity settings this sight performs well in all light conditions.

- Rail System - Possibly the most versatile, and arguably the most popular, accessory of this rifle platform is a front rail system that allows for the attachment of numerous accessories. Since this was a project utilizing a base rifle with a standard upper receiver and front sight post, a TDI Arms X6 rail system was chosen. Manufactured from solid billet aviation aluminum, this 2-piece, 6-rail system simply replaces a standard carbine-length handguard and works in conjunction with the standard front sight. It is a drop-on rail installed with the factory delta ring and tightened with 5 bolts to secure the system. The top MIL-STD 1913 rail matches the height of the factory flat top rail to facilitate multiple accessories. Unused rail surfaces were covered with the assistance of an X6 Thermal Rail Cover Kit.

- Front Vertical Grip - The particular grip chosen for this project met a few different criteria. We used a CAA Flashlight Grip Adapter. This vertical front grip mounts on the front rail and accepts a standard 1-inch flashlight. Tactical lights with a rear button can utilize the built-in thumb switch in both a constant on and a momentary on mode. Lights with a pigtail-style pressure switch are also accommodated with built-in mounting surfaces.

The front handguard was replaced with a TDI Arms X6 Rail Mount. It simply takes the place of the factory, carbine handguard and uses the delta ring. It is a 2-piece handguard and is secured with 5 bolts for rigidity. There are 4 rails in the standard 3, 6, 9 and 12 o'clock positions as well as 2 smaller rails on each side of the front site post for other accessories. This rail gave us the ability to easily attach the S.P.O.T. Red-Dot sight and the vertical front grip.

Enough is Enough

Since we earlier made light of those who over-accessorize their rifles, we were cautious not to fall into that category with this build. Those who either need more accessories or just different accessories can rest well knowing that we didn't even scratch the surface of the available items. For a full listing of CAA accessories you can visit their website at www.commandarms.com. Be prepared to be there for a while. There are numerous variants of the items we installed such as stocks, grips, mounts, slings and several other accessories not included such as magazine clamps, stock accessories, lasers and mounts, bipods and much more. They also carry accessories for many more firearms than just AR-15 style guns including AK47s, Uzis, P-90s, MP5s, Galils and several handguns.

Solid Billet AR-15 Style Receivers

Approximately 15 miles east of Phoenix, Arizona is the city of Mesa. Boasting an average of 313 days of sunshine every year, it is only appropriate that a business located in the southwest desert, manufacturing a version of the Black Rifle, would be called Sun Devil Manufacturing.

Small Arms Review was contacted prior to SAR Show 2005 and invited to tour the Sun Devil Manufacturing facility. David Beaty, the proprietor of Sun Devil Manufacturing, picked us up at the show and drove us to their location in Mesa, less than a 20-minute drive from the Arizona State Fairgrounds. In business for approximately 3 years in their current capacity with the Sun Devil name, Beaty has been working with AR-15 type rifles off and on for almost 20 years.

While talking with Beaty on the way to the shop, it was obvious that he has a great understanding of metals and their properties relating to the firearms manufacturing process. There are several opinions about the quality of methods of manufacture by means of forgings, castings and from solid billet material, and Beaty believes that billet manufactured receivers are superior to the others and that is his reasoning behind the process he utilizes. Beaty believes that a benefit of his billet receivers is that they are much stronger than those manufactured from castings. He also claims the dimensional consistency is much more accurate with billet made receivers than with those built from forgings.

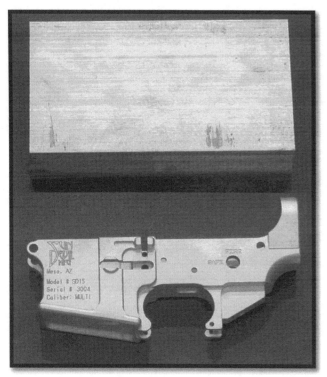

Before and after. Above this finished receiver waiting to go out for anodizing, is an example of the raw billet from which it started.

Upon arriving at the Sun Devil facility we took a brief walking tour beginning with the main machining room. Surrounded by CNC machinery, all performing different tasks, it was easy to see how quality and consistency could be appropriately controlled. Heading to another room we viewed the stacks of raw billet material that would soon be transformed into upper and lower receivers. The material used for the Sun Devil receivers is usually 6061 and are occasionally made from 7075. In yet another room the engraving, inventory and quality control took place. It was an interesting contrast to look at racks of finished products not 10 yards from raw material that had not even been cut to lengths that could yet be easily handled. It is certainly a testimonial to all phases of manufacture being handled in one environment. If everything is not absolutely right, there is no one to point a finger at and Beaty enjoys having complete control over ALL phases of manufacture to ensure the quality he strives for.

When asked what I wanted to see next, the answer was simple: "Let's make a gun." I wanted to start with the raw material and do a photographic run through the entire process for the readers of Small Arms Review. For purposes of proprietary information and tooling, we were asked to skip over a few minor functions. The following is a photographic guide sequence going through the process of transforming a bar of aluminum into a Sun Devil lower receiver.

A second generation lower receiver on the left compared to an early, first generation lower receiver on the right. The new receivers have a raised stippled area on the front of the magazine well and more mass in the front takedown pin lugs.

Sun Devil lower receivers are now actually in their second generation. A first generation receiver can be noticed by the smooth area in front of the magazine well. The second generation receivers have a raised "stippled" pattern in this space. The later receivers also have more material in the front lugs for the takedown pin.

Sun Devil Manufacturing also manufactures their own matched, upper receivers for a perfect fit to their lower receivers. Their upper receivers are immediately noticeable due to their octagonal contour and lack of forward assist mechanism. They also have a 5.75-inch MIL-STD Rail (flat-top) to accommodate a number of scopes, mounts and accessories. They are extremely reinforced and mate to the heavily reinforced area of the buffer tube extension on their lower receivers.

Sun Devil second generation upper receiver and lower receiver prior to assembly.

New Rate Reducing M16/M4 Buffer from MGI

The MGI Rate Reducing Buffer was designed to function in any firearm in the M16 family regardless of stock type or barrel length.

This latest project from MGI is a drop-in unit requiring no tools or additional modification to the firearm; it simply replaces the factory buffer. It is used in conjunction with the factory buffer spring and is not a hydraulic unit, but a mechanical device. As the factory recoil spring is utilized, there is no loss of reliability as a consequence of a weakened charging mechanism use to retard the rate of fire.

The buffer is self-adjusting and will reduce cyclic rate to the lowest possible rate within the parameters of acceptable reliability. The faster your M16 is to begin with, the greater the reduction in rate of fire. This system works both in carbines and in full-length rifles. If the buffer is of the shorter, carbine length, a spacer is included with it for use in a standard A1 or A2 stock.

All testing was performed with the assistance of a PACT MKIV Timer. The PACT MKIV Timer is a small computer you can clip on your belt that will count the number of rounds fired and records the overall time to provide the cyclic rate. It will also record the amount of time between each round. It can be used for competitive shooting when running through a timed course and provide a random buzzer as well. The suggested retail price is under $200.

The MGI Rate Reducing Buffer simply replaces the factory buffer. The factory spring is not changed and no tools are necessary to make the swap.

The first test platform used was an M16 with a collapsible stock and an 11.5-inch barrel. Using standard military 5.56x45mm M193 ball ammo, the average cyclic rate with the factory buffer was 1,029 rpm. When the MGI buffer was installed the cyclic rate dropped to an average of 760 rpm. That is a reduction of 269 rpm. The largest extreme spread was a drop from 1,056 rpm to 745 rpm. That was a cold gun and the reduction was 302 rpm. Using the same gun but running Wolf 55-grain ammunition we averaged 957 rpm with the factory buffer and only 711 rpm with the MGI buffer. That was an average reduction of 246 rpm.

Next, upper receivers were swapped to utilize a 20-inch barrel. The M193 ball averaged 771 rpm with the factory buffer and dropped to 638 rpm with the MGI buffer. The average reduction in cyclic rate in this configuration is 133 rpm. The Wolf ammo averaged 707 rpm with the factory buffer and dropped to 597 rpm with the MGI buffer for an average reduction of 110 rpm.

The third set of tests performed was with a 16-inch barrel chambered in 7.62x39mm. Standard Chicom, steel-cased, Berdan-primed ball ammo was utilized. The original rate of fire with a factory 5.56x45mm buffer averaged 872 rpm. Switching to the MGI buffer dropped the cyclic rate to an average of 685 rpm. That was a decrease in the cyclic rate of 187 rpm. While the reduction was not as great as some of the results with 5.56x45mm ammunition something else started to become very obvious. The perceived recoil was lowered significantly and the muzzle jump was only a fraction of the rise encountered with the original buffer. While this was apparent throughout all the testing, it was more pronounced with the heavier bullet and increased recoil of the 7.62x39mm cartridge.

In order to actually get a close look at what was happening to the muzzle rise, a Nikon CP5000 camera was set up in the movie mode on a tripod. Several strings were fired with the factory buffers as well as the MGI buffer. When we got back to the studio and uploaded the videos, we played them simultaneously and the results were quite revealing. When the factory buffers were being utilized there was a moderate amount of muzzle rise. I have been shooting M16s for many years and I can hold them fairly steady during full-auto bursts. When we viewed the footage of the MGI-buffer-equipped weapons the results were startling. I took a few of these videos, strung them together and uploaded them onto the MGI website. In each video, there is a 20-round burst with a factory buffer followed by a 20-round burst with an MGI buffer. If you put your mouse pointer on the muzzle of the rifle while the video is playing, you can see that while using the standard buffer there is some movement. When the clip with the MGI buffer plays you will notice almost no movement at all. It is especially apparent when using the 20-inch barrel, as the cyclic rate is much slower than the 11.5-inch barrel. If you would like to see these for yourself follow the products link to the MGI Buffer System from the main page at www.mgimilitary.com.

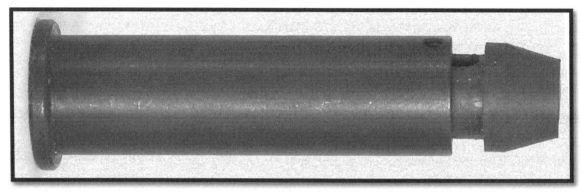

The MGI buffer can easily be identified by the rubber tip that is not flush with the body of the buffer like the originals. When depressed, the tip can be pushed flush to the body, and the spring pressure will return it to its original position when released.

The MGI buffer was tested next with a 9x19mm SMG upper receiver. An 11.5-inch, barreled upper receiver and a Colt-style magazine block were purchased from J&T Distributing. A J&T 9x19mm upper receiver was chosen because it is similar to the original Colt design and uses the standard Colt 9mm magazines. It also permits use of the factory magazine/catch release. While the system runs fine with modified Uzi magazines the testing was performed with original Colt 20-round magazines due to their reputation for reliability. The first string of testing was with the original 5.56x45mm buffer. The average rate of fire was 830 rpm. When the heavy 9mm buffer from J&T was installed, the cyclic rate dropped to 663 rpm. This buffer was replaced by the MGI buffer and the cyclic rate dropped to an average of 622 rpm. All of these 9x19mm tests were duplicated while using a Gemtech 9mm 3-lug adapter and an AWC Minitac suppressor to test the effects the suppressor would have on the cyclic rate, but the results were inconclusive. While the gun functioned well with all three buffers, the sound pressure level was lowered to the extent that the PACT Timer could no longer register every round being fired, yielding false results. Sometimes it would even count "extra" rounds from the SNAP of the bullet hitting the impact area.

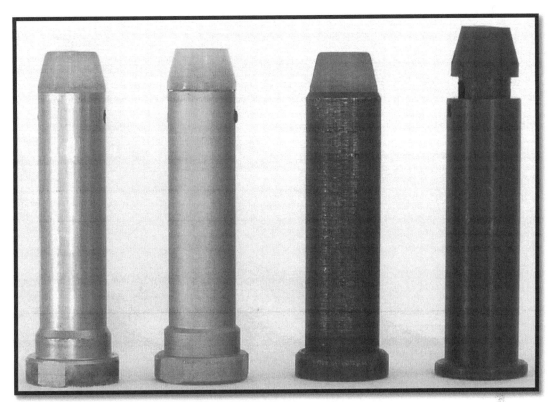

Left to Right: **Factory 5.56x45mm carbine buffer, aftermarket 5.56x45mm carbine buffer, heavy 9x19mm heavy buffer, MGI rate reducing buffer.**

As the 11.5-inch-barreled, 5.56x45mm system had the fastest cyclic rate, as well as the greatest level of reduction in the rate of fire, it was chosen for use during the accuracy testing in fully-auto fire. This was obviously the least controllable platform. All testing thus far has been conducted at 25 yards while shooting a full 20-round magazine in one burst. While not practical in a tactical environment, we felt would provide the greatest test of the actual recoil reduction. Our expectations were confirmed and the hit probability was increased by at least 50% after removing the factory buffer and installing the MGI buffer.

Because of range limitations, we did not test fire in vertical directions. In combat there are sometimes requirements for firing up (Snipers in trees or buildings), or firing down (From helicopter or building). There might be changes in the rate of fire or reliability in those scenarios.

Conclusions

Test firing was conducted in temperatures ranging from over 90ºF to as cold as -5ºF below zero. Functioning was not affected with any buffer used and the reliability remained the same. In every test performed, the cyclic rate was consistently reduced and the recoil spike was cut drastically when the MGI buffer was utilized. Muzzle rise was almost completely eliminated in some of the rifles with longer barrels and was cut significantly in all configurations. In both long and short bursts the hit probability was increased due to the additional controllability. In full-auto, smaller bursts could be fired solely by using a disciplined trigger control with the MGI buffer installed as a result of the significantly reduced cyclic rates. I can recommend the MGI Rate Reducing Buffer without reservations of any kind.

The LM-7: Belt-Fed AR-15/M16 in .22LR

The Radical New Rimfire from Lakeside Machine

The masters of the miniature machine guns have just unveiled their latest creation. In just over a year, from concept to production, Lakeside Machine of Pound, Wisconsin has announced the addition of the LM-7 to their rimfire lineup. The LM-7 is a belt-fed upper receiver chambered in .22 long rifle for an M16 or AR-15 type rifle.

During the ten year period of the Clinton Assault Weapons ban (1994-2004), common firearms that were deemed "assault weapons" were prohibited from manufacture for sale to individuals. Also prohibited were magazines and feeding devices with a capacity greater than ten rounds. This resulted in a cessation of many innovative projects and caused a sharp increase in price for existing supplies of weapons and magazines. There were many new weapon concepts and pioneering ideas during this time, but with a market limited to the military and law enforcement, economically, there was little point in proceeding. With the expiration of the Clinton Assault Weapons ban in 2004, firearm design and ingenuity has reemerged after being stifled for ten years and new designs and products are hitting the market at an amazing pace.

Lakeside Machine has been in the business of manufacturing high capacity rimfire guns since their purchase of Tippmann Arms from F.J. Vollmer and Company in September, 2001. They initially specialized in the manufacture and sales of the one-half scale miniature Tippmann machine guns (Small Arms Review - Vol. 7 No. 6, March 2004). As the 2004 sunset of the ban got closer, their focus switched to a line of newly designed, shoulder-fired variants. Although the firearms could be manufactured in compliance with the ban, the limited availability of belts for feeding them was very poor. With the ban terminated, more belt material was able to be manufactured and a new generation of belt-fed rimfire rifles was born.

The first shoulder fired, belt fed rifle system designed by Lakeside Machine was the BF1 Vindicator (Small Arms Review - Vol. 8 No. 4, January 2005). Introduced in 2004, these rifles were manufactured in .22 Long Rifle with a few chambered in the relatively new .17 Mach II. These rifles used the same cloth belts originally designed for the Tippmann miniature machine guns and can also use the newly designed disintegrating links; another one of Lakeside Machines' recent innovations. The disintegrating links are made of a Nylon material and function with .22LR, .22 Magnum, .17 HMR and .22 Mach II. These links have been upgraded by impregnating them with enough metal content to allow them to be picked up with a magnet.

In October of 2004, Eric Graetz, CEO of Lakeside Machine was approached by a customer and asked if he thought he could design an AR-15/M16 upper receiver that would accept his belts and links. Graetz accepted the challenge. After some months of research and development, the machine shop was retooled to manufacture the latest creation: the LM-7 .22LR (and .17 Mach II) belt-fed upper receiver. The prototype was unveiled in December of 2004 at the SAR Show in Phoenix, Arizona.

The LM-7 (the 7th model firearm developed by Lakeside Machine) is a complete upper receiver assembly that will fit on any standard AR-15 or M16 lower receiver and function with the trigger internals as intended. While offered in a semiautomatic configuration, an upgrade is available so the upper will function in full automatic when used on a registered full automatic lower receiver. To the delight of the NFA community, it will also work in conjunction with a drop-in auto sear.

Mounting the LM-7

Before replacing the stock upper receiver with an LM-7, the factory buffer and spring must be removed from the lower receiver and replaced with the new buffer assembly supplied with the LM-7. The factory hammer spring should also be replaced with a much lighter hammer spring that is also supplied with the LM-7. That is the extent of the modifications to the lower receiver when used on a semiautomatic rifle. When used on a full automatic rifle there are a few timing adjustments that may be necessary and will be discussed later in this article.

Installing the LM-7 upper receiver is as simple as pulling the two takedown pins, removing the factory upper and replacing it with the LM-7 upper receiver. Once pinned on the lower receiver, the factory magazine-well now functions as a brass ejection port. In order to catch the ejected casings, Lakeside Machine supplies a brass catcher that locks into the magazine-well in the same manner as a factory magazine. As it fills to capacity it can simply be "ejected" like a standard magazine, the contents dumped out, and quickly reinserted. The bottom of the brass catcher also has a swing-down floor plate to allow empty brass to flow through when the shooter does not want to retain the ejected casings. The brass catcher doubles as an attachment platform for the optional belt box and link catcher. Shooting long belts without the assistance of an A-Gunner can easily be accomplished with the use of the belt feed box. It holds a little more than 200 belted or linked rounds. Since the links are ejected directly across from the feed tray, another identical box mounted on the opposite side of the feed box catches all the used links.

The LM-7 functions in a similar fashion to a Browning Model 1919 machine gun. It utilizes a shuttle feed mechanism that feeds the belt, extracts each round from the rear of the belt, chambers the round and extracts the empty case after firing. This mechanism does not utilize a locked action. The rifle is loaded by lifting the top cover and inserting the belt with the first round placed below the extractor. The top cover is closed and the gun is charged by pulling the bolt handle back and released one time. As a new round is pulled from the belt and loaded in the chamber the fired case is pushed out of the T-slot in the bolt and dropped into the brass box or directly on the ground.

The LM-7 utilizes an exclusive quick-change barrel (QCB) that can be replaced in seconds. Changing or installing a barrel is as simple as depressing the barrel release button, pulling the barrel strait out, replacing the barrel and releasing the button. It is a direct action that requires no twisting, turning, adjusting or head spacing. Barrels are currently available in two lengths and three styles. Barrel lengths are 16.25 inches and 7.5 inches. The 16.25-inch barrels are contoured just like a standard M4 barrel and can utilize any of the M4 mounting options. Where the barrels are secured in the receiver by the QCB mechanism, they are completely free-floating and will work fine with any free-floating style handguard. If you wish to use standard M4 handguards you can utilize an adapter that secures them at the front and also doubles as a front sight block. Where it is unnecessary for the front of the barrel to be supported by any handguard mounting hardware, it lends itself well to the use of shorter barrels with sound suppressors. The 7.5-inch barrel we were shooting with was often fitted with an AWC MKII suppressor that protruded less than 4 inches past the standard carbine handguards. If this system were going to be set up in this configuration for regular use, the handguard would certainly be replaced with a free-floating type or any of the rail systems allowing the use of various accessories.

On the rear of the top cover is a 4.25-inch M1913 Picatinny rail to accept short optics or a removable rear sight. The front block installed with a 16-inch barrel includes a 1.75-inch rail that can host standard removable front sights and accessories. The LM-7 we tested was equipped with an EO Tech Model 552 Holographic Sight. While the version using AA batteries was a little long on this mount, it was certainly still usable. While using the sight with multiple quick-change barrels, we noticed very little point of impact change. Each LM-7 system is shipped with the LM-7 Buffer System, a 16.25-inch barrel, front sight block, brass catcher, two feed boxes, two 100-round belts and 200 links.

Rimfire Ammo Reliability

When the LM-7 was designed, it was built to function with the inexpensive CCI Blazer ammunition. This is fantastic news for shooters who are conscientious about their ammo budget. We tested the LM-7 with several types of .22LR ammunition and have included a chart indicating performance, muzzle velocity and rate of fire when utilized in full automatic. The ammunition we tested included CCI Blazer, CCI Mini-Mag, CCI Stinger, Remington Thunderbolt, Federal Lightning, Federal Bulk Pack, Federal Champion, and Winchester Wildcat. It ran fine with most but the Federal Champion was the least reliable. The absolute best was the CCI Stinger due to the increased power over standard .22LR ammo but the additional cost (almost $4.00 for a box of 50) may be enough to discourage many people. The Winchester Wildcat, Federal Lightning and CCI Blazer all worked great. The Federal Bulk Pack and Remington Thunderbolt also worked quite reliably. For some reason it was a little finicky with the CCI Mini-Mags. The author has found after years of shooting select-fire rimfire rifles and pistols, that when determining which .22LR ammo will work the best, it is usually a good idea to just try several brands in your own firearm. Some seem to run great with one particular brand while other firearms like something completely different. Factors that may be important in the LM-7 that would not necessarily be an issue in other .22LR guns include the thickness of the rim. After extraction from the belt, the round is channeled down a T-slot to the chamber, and captured in the T-Slot again as it is channeled down to the point of ejection. If a particular brand or batch of ammo has a thicker than usual rim, it could interfere with, or stop, the operation of the gun altogether.

The greatest obstacle in reliable functioning is the lack of energy in the little .22LR cartridge. It takes a lot of energy to run these machines in full automatic and when you start adding factors like pulling belts and links, the challenge gets even greater. Light parts and springs, necessary because of the low amount of energy created by the rimfire round, only add to bolt bounce problems and pose additional hurdles in the development of select-fire, Rimfire guns. Unlike many other select-fire .22 LR firearms, bolt bounce is not a problem in the LM-7 due to the function of the extractor pulling the new round from the belt at the same time the chambered round is fired. This action dampens the rearward travel of the bolt and eliminates the bolt bounce issue.

Several brands of .22LR ammo were tested in the LM7.

Timing and Function in Full Automatic

With the weak .22LR ammo in mind, we can get into some of the timing issues when shooting the LM-7 in full automatic. Subtle inconsistencies that are not critical dimensions with higher-powered rounds can often be the determining factor in creating problems when shooting rimfire rifles. In the case of the LM-7, some of the loose tolerances of standard 5.56mm guns combined with the fact there are several manufacturers of rifles, receivers and parts to fill them, create an enormous number of potential combinations.

When shooting the LM-7, the trigger function is identical to that of the original 5.56mm rifle. While shooting in semiautomatic mode, when the bolt carrier recoils from shooting the chambered round, the hammer is cocked and held captive by the disconnector. When the shooter lets off the trigger the hammer releases from the disconnector and engages the front of the trigger. When the shooter squeezes the trigger the hammer is released and the process starts all over again. When shooting in full automatic mode, the hammer bypasses the disconnector and does not contact it at all. A spur on the back of the hammer is caught and held captive by the auto sear and it is only released when the bolt carrier trips that sear when the gun has chambered the new round and it is in battery. The timing aspect comes into play with the relationship between the bolt carrier sear trip and the sear releasing the hammer.

The part of the LM-7 that has to be altered for full automatic fire is the bolt carrier. Just like the stand-

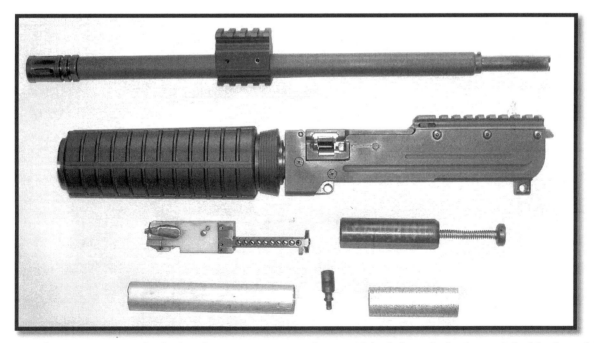

The complete LM7 system includes the new upper receiver, a 16-inch barrel, the front sight block, carbine length handguards, LM7 bolt and bolt handle, LM7 recoil assembly and both recoil assembly spacers.

ard AR-15 and M16, all that is necessary for the upper receiver to accommodate a legally owned full automatic lower receiver, is the addition of a sear trip on the carrier. Lakeside Machine will be happy to provide owners of registered receivers or drop in auto sears with the piece needed to engage the auto sear. That is where the timing comes into play. The sear trip on the carrier needs to contact the auto sear at the precise time the new round is fully chambered. Due to the large number of parts and receivers on the market, one gun may need a specific thickness on the sear trip to engage the sear at the correct time while another gun needs one much thicker. This timing can be accomplished by simply removing an Allen-head screw, removing the sear trip, adding a piece of shim material (an old feeler gauge set works great for shimming) and replacing the trip and screw. When the hammer drops at the same time the bolt completely closes it is ready to go.

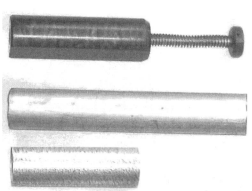

Early in the testing we realized the tolerance difference in some hammers also created a problem where the guns would not cock the hammer far enough to catch it under the auto sear. This would cause the hammer to follow the carrier back into battery without firing it. Some of the hammer spurs were much thicker and/or longer than others. The cause of the problem was the lower power of the .22LR ammo was sending the much lighter bolt carrier back much slower than a standard 5.56mm carrier and not getting the hammer to fall back far enough. The reason this is not usually a problem with the 5.56mm round is because the mass of the carrier and the speed it is recoiling at is much greater than that of the LM-7. Lowering the internals of the entire LM-7 system so the hammer would

The LM7 recoil assembly replaces the factory buffer and buffer spring. The same assembly is used for both carbine and full-length stocks in conjunction with the correct length spacer supplied by Lakeside Machine.

drop much lower and not rely on speed, but simply movement, solved this issue.

Loading Belts

If there is any downfall to shooting belt fed firearms it is the simple fact that we have to load belts before we can shoot them. Lakeside Machine has helped us out a little in this area with the introduction of their new belt-loading device. A box of ammo, or small handful if you have bulk ammo, is dumped into the sorting hopper. A few shakes of the wrist and several are all lined up protruding from a small slot in the bottom of the device. A transfer bar is pushed up through the slot, catching the already lined up ammo, and slid out the front of the hopper. The transfer bar is then inserted into a loading block and the result is 10 rounds, all perfectly spaced and ready to be belted. When the belt is pushed over the rounds in the loading block they are all perfectly spaced and seated to the correct depth when the belt is removed. Several loading blocks can even be connected in unison to speed up the process. The author uses 3 blocks mounted together and has found that to be fast and comfortable.

Since new belts are very tight the first time they are loaded, there is a spike that acts as a belt spreader included with the loading tool that can be mounted with the loading blocks. A simple pass through each pocket prior to loading each first round and it is no longer a struggle. No more blistered fingers from loading new belts and more time shooting instead of loading. As previously mentioned, you can also use disintegrating links instead of the cloth belts. These are much easier to load but don't tend to hold the linked ammo quite as secure as the cloth belts do. Some people have found that given a slight pinch while loading them creates a little tighter hold. Both belts and links provide excellent results at the range. The 8-piece belt loading system is available for $40 and should be mandatory equipment for anyone who owns one of the Tippmann miniatures, a Vindicator Carbine or an LM-7.

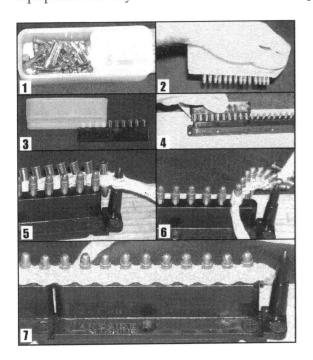

The belt loading set makes the loading of belts much easier. The hopper holds a full box of .22LR ammo. It is just dumped in and the cover closed. With your finger over the front slot, shake the hopper back and forth a few times and the ammo falls down and aligns itself in the loading slot. Using the transfer bar, line up the first round and push the bar up into the slot of the hopper. Slide the transfer bar forward out the slot, and it will be filled with 10 rounds. Line the transfer bar up with a loading block and tip it upside down. The loading block will then be filled with ammo, perfectly spaced at the correct depth for placement in the belt. If you are filling a new belt, run each loop over the spike to stretch it out. The stretched loop will easily drop over a round in the loading block. To check the belts for proper depth before firing, it may be inserted into a series of loading blocks and seated into proper placement.

BATFE Technology Branch Ruling

Unlike many other manufacturing projects, there was still something necessary even when the majority of the in-house troubleshooting had been completed. The Technology Branch of the Bureau of Alcohol, Tobacco Firearms and Explosives makes legal determinations on new firearms and related accessories based on samples submitted. They examine these new designs and based on the item submitted they will issue a determination in writing. There have been other designs submitted for determination changing the caliber and/or feed mechanism of specific firearms, where the devices were ruled firearms of themselves. There have been other designs where Technology Branch has determined the new device was too easily convertible to full automatic fire and ruled as machine guns, themselves. For obvious legal reasons a sample LM-7 was submitted to ATF and on December 6, 2005 it was determined that the LM-7 does NOT meet the definition of a firearm or a machine gun, and is simply an upper receiver, like countless other replacement upper receivers on the market.

Range Performance

Most of the range time was during sub-freezing temperatures at our production office in Maine. The LM-7 ran perfect in semiautomatic mode right from the box. In order to achieve reliable performance in full automatic, it had to be timed. This can be accomplished in less than an hour with the right materials and depending on the firearm you have, it may not involve any adjustments at all. As explained above, during preliminary testing we discovered several variables in most lower receiver fire control groups that had to be tweaked, and at this point Lakeside Machine has already addressed them in their new production models. Once we had everything adjusted and timed it ran excellent. We successfully ran several long belts just for function testing (ok, and a little fun) and fired several strings collecting data on muzzle velocity and rate of fire with several types of ammo in different configurations. The data from those tests are provided in the accompanying charts.

Conclusion

Lakeside Machine has hit a home run with this design. As an accessory for a military style firearm that has been the USA primary service weapon for over 40 years, there are a lot of host guns out there as potential customers. It is a reasonably priced way for a shooter to "upgrade" to a belt-fed firearm and it is a great way to shoot on a budget with the cheap price of most .22LR ammunition. It is fun to shoot and works excellent right out of the box in semiautomatic mode and, with a minimal amount of timing and fine-tuning, in full automatic. The conversion to LM-7 from a factory upper receiver is simple and can be completed in less than a minute. The vast number of accessories available for the LM-7, both from Lakeside Machine and current ones already on the market create an infinite number of configurations to suit any shooter. Where the LM-7 works in conjunction with previously owned, registered M16s and drop-in auto sears, it is about as close to having a "new" machine gun as we can get since May 19, 1986. There will always be room in this writer's reference collection for an LM-7.

.22LR Rate of Fire

Barrel Length Ammunition	16.12-inches w/flash hider	16.25-inches w/sound suppressor
Remington Thunderbolt	970rpm	1,025rpm
CCI Mini Mag	1,046rpm	1,036rpm
CCI Stinger	1,076rpm	1,085rpm
Federal Bulk Pack	975rpm	N/A
Federal Champion	857rpm	857rpm

Measurements recorded with a PACT MKIV Timer & Chronograph.

.22 Long Rifle Muzzle Velocity

Barrel Length Ammunition	7.5-inches w/flash hider	7.5-inches w/sound suppressor	16.25-inches w/flash hider	16.25-inches w/sound suppressor
Remington Thunderbolt	997fps	1,032fps	1,095fps	1,088fps
CCI Mini Mag	975fps	1,027fps	1,069fps	1,055fps
CCI Stinger	1,334fps	1,345fps	1,450fps	1,474fps
Federal Bulk Pack	1,064fps	1,054fps	1,139fps	1,148fps
Federal Champion	1,111fps	1,141fps	1,179fps	1,206fps

Measurements recorded 8 feet in front of the muzzle with a PACT MKIV Timer & Chronograph

The QCB Upper Receiver for the AR-15/M16/M4

The QCB (Quick Change Barrel) M16 Upper Receiver is one of the most radical modifications to the AR-15/M16/M4 weapons system that the author has seen to date. While I am not aware of any other weapon system with so many options, accessories and available configurations, the list of options continues to grow at an amazing pace. There are countless manufacturers who have products and upgrades for this family of firearms, from muzzle brakes to custom stocks and every piece in between. Some are simple attachments and enhancements such as grips and scope mounts, and others are so radical that the rifle hardly even resembles the original "Black Rifle" anymore. The MGI QCB Upper Receiver falls into the latter category, in both design and function.

An MGI QCB equipped M16 with the barrel removed.

Quick-change barrel mechanisms are common in machine guns but are more of a rarity in assault rifles. Examples of QCB systems in larger machine guns would include the M60, the Stoner 63 Rifles, M249, the M240 and the M2HB-QCB by FN-Herstal. The newer M96 Expeditionary Rifle by Robinson Armament also utilizes a QCB similar to the Stoner 63 System it was based on.

Mack Gwinn, the designer of the M2HB-QCB, designed this latest addition to the QCB family. Having over 25 firearms related patents, and founding several firearms companies including Bushmaster and MWG, Gwinn is far from a newcomer to the world of gun design. MGI Military currently offers several upgrades for the M16 weapons system. Their product line includes a rate-reducing buffer, regulated gas tubes, the D-Fender D-Ring and will soon be offering a new lower receiver with interchangeable magazine wells, allowing the user to use common magazines in different calibers. Other products in line for production also include open-bolt firing mechanisms and an open-bolt/closed-bolt mechanism. (Watch future issues of SAR for a feature on these once they are in production).

A major advantage of the M16 weapons system is the modular design. Using one lower receiver as a platform, the part the BATF considers the firearm; the owner can effectively have several different rifles just by purchasing new parts. Generally, most of these parts, regardless of manufacturer, are interchangeable with little or no modification. This, combined with the fact that it has been a primary service rifle for over 40 years and

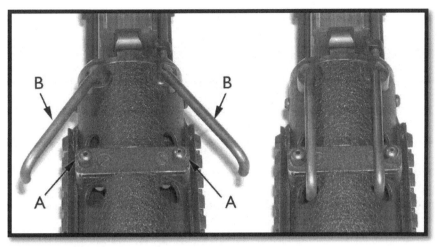

Changing a barrel is as easy as depressing the barrel release lever retainer (A) and swinging open the barrel release lever (B). The old barrel is removed, the new barrel is inserted and the levers are closed until they snap into place.

there is a huge inventory of surplus parts, makes it extremely easy to maintain and reconfigure as desired. This huge inventory of parts was not overlooked when the MGI QCB was designed. As radically different as it looks and performs, it actually uses standard barrels. All the owner has to do is remove the original delta ring, barrel nut, sling swivel and front handguard keeper and it is then completely compatible with the MGI QCB upper receiver. This means no expensive, custom or additional proprietary barrels to buy and can be used immediately with all your standard barrels. While none of these changes are permanent, the barrels can always be reconfigured to attach to the factory, standard upper receiver again.

Presently, all MGI QCB upper receivers are manufactured in a flat-top configuration. A 6-inch, MIL-STD-1913 rail interface is mounted on top of the receiver in place of the standard carry handle. On the handguard, there are three more MIL-STD-1913 rails for attaching accessories: a 6-inch rail at the 3 o'clock and 9 o'clock positions and a 2-inch rail at 6 o'clock. The receiver is based on the M16 design utilizing the small front takedown pin so it is completely compatible with all M16s and most AR-15s. Some of the Colt AR-15s use a larger front takedown pin so a reverse offset pin is necessary to replace the factory one.

With an overall length of only 15 inches, the MGI QCB upper receiver gives the shooter the advantage of having an extremely compact rifle. For comparison, a standard upper receiver with a 16-inch barrel is almost 25 inches long. Utilizing an MGI QCB upper receiver, a complete M16 or AR-15, including a 16-inch barrel, with upper receiver, lower receiver and optics can actually fit completely in a standard briefcase. This gives a professional operator such as a bodyguard or special-ops member an amazing amount of firepower in a smaller package than ever before.

To install a barrel in the MGI QCB Upper Receiver, all you do is push down on the spring-loaded barrel release lever retainer, swing out the release levers, insert the barrel, and close the barrel release levers until they snap into place. Barrel changes are accomplished in only seconds. The shooter can be afforded the luxury of having several barrels for different applications that can be changed faster than ever before. Caliber changes are made with ease without the burden and expense of needing additional upper receivers.

The finish on the handguard portion of the MGI QCB upper receiver is a non-glare black phosphate and is made from aluminum keeping the unit lightweight. There are 24 circular cooling vents giving the handguard a similar appearance to a Browning M1919 barrel shroud. The handguard is attached to the upper receiver and is completely free-floating, transferring absolutely no tension on the barrel.

All units are personally test fired by MGI staff before shipping and are guaranteed to function with your standard barrels. Test groups are fired and the barrels are removed. The barrels are reinstalled and test fired again to confirm continuity in the grouping. The rifle will only be as accurate as the shooter, the barrel and the ammunition combination will allow, but the group placement always returns upon disassembly and reassembly of the barrel and upper receiver.

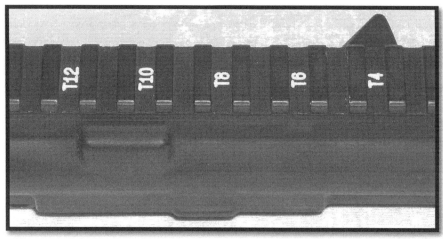

The MGI QCB upper receiver is topped with a 6" MIL-STD 1913 rail interface, clearly marked for precise placement of accessories.

During test firing, the author utilized several barrels with absolutely no failure to function with any of them. For purposes of testing different calibers, 5.56x45mm, 7.62x39mm and .22LR were used. A custom 9-inch, dedicated .22LR barrel was used for that caliber, combined with one of Jonathan Ciener's .22LR Atchisson kits. It functioned without any problems in both semiautomatic and full automatic. Where no gas tube is necessary in the .22LR configuration, a standard barrel may be cut very short without regard to the gas block. The gas block is no longer necessary as a method of handguard attachment so the length of the barrel is determined by the user's imagination.

One thing to note when changing barrels is the bolt carrier must be locked in the rearward position before attempting to remove a barrel. The locking lugs of the bolt otherwise engage the locking mechanism holding the barrel firmly in place. With the Atchisson .22LR kit, the lack of locking lugs may lead you to believe that the barrel can be removed without locking the bolt carrier rearward. However, the bolt hold-open device does not function with the Atchisson kit due to its short cycle, and it was discovered that when the barrel was removed with the kit installed, the kit would slide forward with the buffer often following it. The result was usually a jammed up rifle. It is recommended that if you are utilizing an Atchisson .22LR kit, it should be removed before changing barrels in the MGI QCB upper receiver.

Conclusion

The author, being a big fan of the M16 weapons system, has had the opportunity to test a countless number of enhancements, attachments and upgrades in the past. Only a few have been as drastically altered from the original design as the MGI QCB upper receiver. Some have been manufactured to look different but this enhancement has been designed to function entirely different. The ability to change barrels so fast and easy gives the shooter an added flexibility over the original design. Configuring your rifle for different tasks can now be accomplished in seconds. A shooter can go from a light barrel to a heavy barrel and from a short barrel to a long barrel in lightning speed utilizing the MGI QCB upper receiver.

The decrease in size when the barrel is removed provides a much smaller package than the original system, giving operators more storage options than before.

The end user now has the option of purchasing spare barrels without needing spare upper receivers. This keeps the expense of barrel and caliber changes to a minimum.

Cleaning the barrel, especially the chamber and locking area, have never been easier. Now that completely removing the barrel to get at this section only involves throwing a couple of levers and a spare second or two, the user can maintain his weapon system better than ever before.

The unit tested by SAR for this evaluation performed exactly as the manufacturer claimed it would and exceeded the expectations of the author. With a suggested retail price of $550.00 (barrel and bolt with carrier not included), the MGI QCB upper receiver provides the serious AR-15 / M16 collector and shooter opportunities never before possible. As of this writing, units were in stock and shipping regularly.

Belt-fed Black Rifle

The Black Rifle community is as diverse as the number of optional available weapon configurations: and that number is quickly heading towards infinite. Opinions run deep on topics such as effective barrel lengths, gas systems, accessories and even calibers. While most just boil down to personal preference with few real "wrong answers;" those who harbor these opinions are passionate and serious. One thing that most people who are hard-core, life-long fans of the AR-15/M16/M4 weapons system DO have in common is a zeal for early designs and obscure configurations. The early belt-fed black rifle designs may indeed be the Holy Grail of this system and Small Arms Review is pleased to have obtained an original Colt/Ciener AR-15 H-Bar to examine.

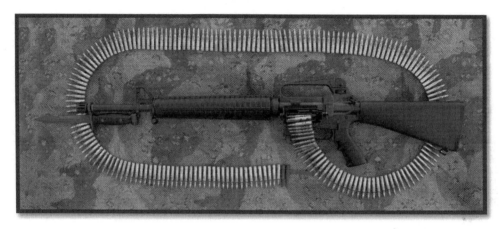

In the Beginning

In the late 1950s, Eugene Stoner and his engineers at ArmaLite had the idea to try a belt-feed unit chambered in .308 on one of his AR-10 designs. While the system indeed worked, and the U.S was actively searching for a new system of this sort, the idea was never actually brought to production. The Dutch AR-10 programs experimented further with the belt-fed AR-10. A little later, the Colt Firearms experimental group toyed with the idea of scaling the system down for 5.56x45mm to be hosted on one of the early AR-15 platforms. Under the supervision of Rob Roy, they produced less than a dozen prototype guns, all slightly different, but the project was eventually abandoned for over 20 years while designs went in the direction of the standard magazine-fed guns we are all familiar with today, which has ended up as the primary weapon system for the United States military for several decades. There is a lot of speculation, and many theories, why the belt-fed AR-15 never took off in those early days and most revolve around the deep interest in "upgrading" to the more potent and powerful 7.62x51 NATO cartridge.

The ammunition is not fed in the familiar "brass to grass" manner. Since the rounds are stripped from the link from the top, just like being fed from a magazine, the link must be on the bottom.

Fast Forward to the Mid 1980s

Jonathan Arthur Ciener had been manufacturing machine guns and sound suppressors since the mid-1970s, and his products have become a staple in the Class III industry. Best known at the time for his silencers, he was producing quality (and very effective) suppressors with an interest in the civilian market; an area that received little attention at the time. While many other legendary manufacturers in our community were engaged in the military weapons market at the same time, most were working in the direction of the sacred U.S. Government contract and the recreational and civilian shooters remained a very small percentage of the overall manufacturing and marketing plans of the era.

While not all alone, Jonathan Ciener was standing tall in his efforts of actively designing, manufacturing and marketing silencers and machine guns for the civilian market. Few of us who were an active part of the "Gun Culture" during the early 1980s will forget the red and white, multi-page catalogs published by Ciener, as they were an important piece of reference literature and used to introduce thousands of civilian shooters to the availability of these firearms. While the pages were filled with many of Ciener's offerings in the suppressor arena, there were also pages of his machine guns, grenade launchers and related accessories. They explained the legalities of owning these firearms and devices and included retail pricing for those interested in purchasing them. Many were indeed considered "wish-books" and collected like fine literature. In the late 1980s (or perhaps early 1990s) there was a 2-page spread added to the latest catalog, which included and detailed the newly available Belt-

Fed AR-15. Ciener's first product offerings were "kits" to make your own Belt-Fed AR-15, but eventually he offered the complete service.

For the first time in the civilian market a currently produced belt-fed semiautomatic firearm was offered for sale, and the platform was the tried and true AR-15. This was also the first time a belt-fed firearm was offered to the public in the United States, chambered in .223 (5.56x45mm).

Same Thing, Just Different

With several differences from other available belt-fed firearms, the most unique feature may have actually been the lack of a top cover and additional top mounted feed mechanism such as that used by almost every other system of the time. Immediately recognizable from previous belt-fed designs including Maxim and Browning machine guns, the German MG34 and MG42 guns, the M60 and even the M249 SAW and M240 GPMG, there is no top cover, and like on a few of them, no roller assisted track feed mechanism above the action of the Ciener Belt-Fed AR-15.

The actual feeding and firing function of the Ciener gun very closely mimics the original black rifle, stripping the rounds from the belt in the same manner as stripping the rounds from a standard bottom loaded box magazine and fired from the same closed bolt. The mechanism works so close to the original design that without the use of any tools the belt-feed mechanism can be removed and the gun would still function perfectly when fed from a normal box magazine, regardless of the capacity. With the Ciener conversion, the gun is completely backwards compatible to allow the use of both standard box magazines and the new belt-feed system.

How DOES it Work?

Since there is no top cover and no standard shuttle feed mechanism, the gun needs to harness the energy from somewhere else. Like many others, the rearward motion of the bolt carrier is still harnessed to provide the energy to pull the belt into the action but it is captured on the side of the bolt instead of the top. There is an angled slot milled into the left side of the bolt carrier which captures a steel pin that travels through the outside of the upper receiver to the exterior drive unit. When the belt-feed mechanism is installed, (simply inserted into the magazine-well of an open lower receiver) it connects to this sliding drive unit with a spring-loaded pawl lock for easy installation and removal.

The belt-fed mechanism out of the firearm. This is the presentation of the round as it is ready to be stripped and chambered. As far as the bolt is concerned, it is just another round coming from a magazine pushed up and in place by a follower. A light piece of spring steel (A) lifts the front of the round for proper alignment and the slotted link (B) holds the round on an interior tooth so it is sturdy from both sides as it is chambered as normal.

Looking inside the feed mechanism when it is installed will reveal 4 spring-loaded feed pawls. There are two on the top and two on the bottom. These pawls cam up and down as the mechanism rocks (in a see-saw motion) caused from the exterior drive lifting and lowering the linkage as the bolt carrier moved from front to rear and back again. These pawls pull, than hold the belted ammo in the mechanism in sequence as it rocks back and forth. Just like the unmodified rifle, it fires from a closed bolt so a round may be loaded and ready to fire in situations where such a condition is desired and determined safe.

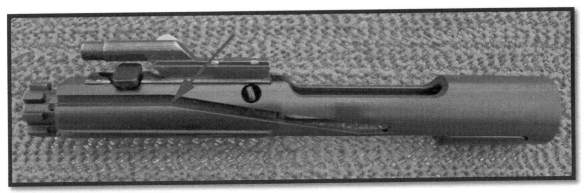

The original bolt carrier is almost unaltered except for the addition of an angled cam slot cut into the left side of the carrier. The slot is angled down toward the rear of the bolt carrier to "drive" the exterior drive unit as it moves to the rear and the front.

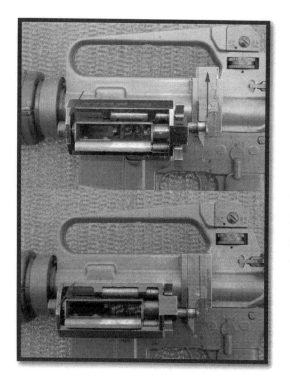

With the mechanism installed and ready to fire, it is easy to see how the belt pull mechanism functions. As the bolt carrier moves to the rear after being fired (top), the exterior drive unit lifts up causing the feed unit to rock down. As the bolt carrier returns to the front, the exterior drive unit lowers causing the feed unit to rock up in the back. It is this "see-saw" motion that gives the four interior feed pawls the ability to capture, pull, and retain the belt as it is fired.

Upon further examination of the feed mechanism, a small piece of spring steel can be seen to the front of the feed pawls. This creates a light but steady amount of lift necessary for proper round presentation for reliable feeding. As mentioned previously the round is presented to the bolt carrier and bolt just as if it is being fed from an inserted magazine.

As the round is stripped from the link and chambered, the belt advances from the motion caused by the cam slot on the forward moving bolt carrier and the empty link advances out and into the link chute or onto the ground. Since the links are modified XM27 (M249/Minimi) links and VERY expensive to purchase as modified, it is suggested to use the link chute.

The link modification is a precise slot that exposes almost 1/2 the diameter of the round. Looking inside the mechanism for a short time, this "head scratcher" of a modification turns into an incredibly logical and necessary step. Since the belt is fed from the side and presented for feeding from the bottom (like a standard magazine) it is missing the stability and support of the feed lips of an actual magazine that holds the round perfectly in line with the chamber as it is stripped by the bolt. Since it is only supported on the side by the link and held up on the front it has a tendency to twist to the left as it is being pushed from the link. This would cause an immediate feeding problem due to the unsupported alignment. Colt solved this issue by adding a small tooth to the link chute, which acts as a "feeding boss" holding the link from the right when the slot from the previous link slides over the tooth. This gives the round a strait and stable platform to sit in while being chambered. This "boss" tooth is part of the drop-in feed mechanism and not the collection chute so for those less concerned with collecting these links it is possible to use it without the box.

Ciener's AR-15 Modifications

When the Ciener belt-fed AR-15 and M16 was introduced, purchasers had the option of purchasing one off the shelf or sending their original Colt rifle in for the necessary modifications. The work is extensive to the original gun and it is far from a drop-in conversion. As previously mentioned though, once the conversion is completed the belt-feed mechanism can easily be removed to use the rifle with standard magazines.

The upper receiver is modified by removing material to allow the feed mechanism to fit in the gun and the exterior drive unit is installed. The bolt carrier is slotted to intercept the steel cam pin, which connects to the linkage in the belt-feed unit once installed in the lower receiver. The lower receiver is also modified by removing material to accept the belt-feed mechanism. The rifle will function normally with a standard magazine but these receiver modifications will act as "windows" allowing the user to see a portion of the magazine when using it in this manner. Even after it is modified a standard upper receiver may be used with the lower receiver functioning like a factory gun was intended. If the Ciener upper is to be used with a standard box magazine, the modified bolt carrier must still be used due to the addition of the steel cam pin.

Inserting and removing the belt-feed mechanism is as simple as opening the rifle in the normal fashion. The rear takedown pin is pushed through and the upper is opened by rotating on the front takedown pin. The belt-feed mechanism is dropped into the mag-well and automatically lined up for closing. As the upper is closed onto the lower, the spring-loaded pawl lock is depressed and allowed to spring back into the exterior drive unit on the upper receiver. To remove the mechanism, it is done in reverse order starting with depressing the spring-loaded pawl lock.

The bottom of the belt-feed mechanism extends past the bottom of the mag-well to act as the attachment point for the belt feed box and link chute. The box has a separate compartment to hold the fired links so they do not mix with the belted ammunition. The box can be removed by one of two methods. It is secured to the bottom of the feed mechanism with a single pushpin. It can either be removed completely by pulling and removing the pin or a toggle switch can be rotated on the right side of the box allowing just the bottom to slide off to the left for emptying and refilling leaving the link chute attached to the gun. The latter is much easier when a simple reload is in order.

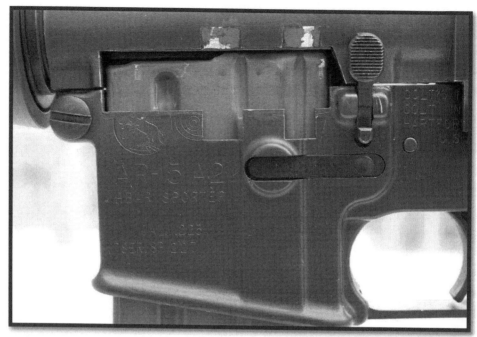

When the belt feed unit is removed, a standard magazine can be used with the Colt/Ciener conversion. The modifications necessary for the fitting of the belt feed mechanism create "windows" in the action when a standard magazine is used. This is the left-side view and the most heavily modified side of the receiver.

Live Fire

The first order is to link the ammo and fill the feed box. Ammo is pressed into the links until it snaps into place. At the end of the belt should be an end tab which consists of 2 dummy rounds and a 2.25-inch tab. The end tab allows the bolt to be held open upon firing the last round, which would not happen since there is no "follower" as in a conventional box magazine.

Unlike many other belt-fed firearms, the ammo is loaded with the links down instead of the normal "brass to grass" protocol. This is so the links are on the bottom and the rounds are pushed over them just like being pushed up and out of a box magazine.

To insert the belt, the bolt carrier needs to be locked back. This is a BIG issue of concern because if the entire system has any flaws at all, this is it. Reading close here can save the user a lot of embarrassment and a fair amount of pain. The bolt release is concealed behind the belt-feed mechanism when it is installed and caution must be used anytime this is engaged. NEVER, at any time, should the user hit the bolt release with anything considered essential equipment (like fingers or a thumb) when the bolt is back! (Yes, this writer knows this from first-hand stupidity, er... ah... I mean experience).

With the bolt back we inserted the belt (links down) until it clicked twice. A view inside the dust cover revealed the round properly seated for feeding with the groove in the link engaged in the tooth portion of the link chute. With a small tug on the charging handle the bolt was slammed home and in battery.

The day was started with a quantity of Federal XM193 ammo, all of which ran without so much as a glitch. After a small rear sight adjustment we shot 10-round groups for hours switching between 3 shooters. Factory A2 sights were all we used and the distance was approximately 60 yards. Since the purpose of the testing was for function, we were satisfied with the distance and sight combination as multiple 2-inch and 3-inch groups were repeated throughout the afternoon. After we exhausted the Federal ammo we linked a fair quantity of Wolf Polyformance ammunition and repeated the process. The groups were the same and the only malfunction we encountered was a failure to feed with what turned out to be a bent link.

It will be interesting in the future to mount some optics and shoot for accuracy at a proper distance but it wasn't on the agenda for this test. What was noticed was the consistency of the ejected casings. We were running 50-round belts all from the box, and one shooter commented that we could have placed a coffee can 3 feet from the bench in a 4 o'clock position and have caught about 98% of the empty casings. Amazingly enough they all looked as though they were being "policed" throughout the day just because of the pile they were in getting higher and higher.

After each belt would empty, the bolt carrier would CAREFULLY be locked back, and the ears releasing the pawls were depressed to remove the end tab and dummy rounds. This would leave it ready for the next reload.

Conclusion

Without a doubt, this is a gun that should still be in production. We have no idea if it would be price prohibitive to manufacture or what the market would be, but we know that everyone who has handled this has been extremely impressed and envious. The quality of this gun is nothing short of amazing and it is obvious the first time the charging handle is pulled back and the glass-smooth action is felt. The parts are true poetry in motion for something so radically different from the original design.

Having a flawlessly running example that was spawned from such an important era in the wonder years of "modern" firearms designs is almost priceless. When handling this gun it is impossible not to think of "what could have been" during these sensitive trials and test periods that gave us the designs we have today.

This is the place we would usually list the manufacturer's information and suggested retail pricing, but since these guns have long been unavailable, we won't irritate Mr. Ciener by adding his current contact information here. He has been out of the belt-fed AR business for a long time and specializes today in .22 LR subcaliber units for several modern firearms. We have heard though that he may have just a few of these left in inventory from years ago, and if you do happen to run into him it may be worth asking if they are for sale.

Valkyrie Armament, LLC's Belt-fed Conversion

The Valkyrie Armament BSR-MOD-1 rifle utilizes proven systems from the past and integrates new upgrades and adaptations to modern firearms in the black rifle family.

The Valkyrie BSR-Mod1 combines the simplicity and technology of the early, original ArmaLite/Colt belt-fed AR-15 designs with today's modern materials and manufacturing methods to provide end users with an accessory they have desired for years. The ability to have your own AR-15 type rifle converted for a reasonable price and back in your hands in under a month.

Those of us who are heavily involved with military-style rifles live in a universe where new accessories are created for many popular platforms with extreme speed. Thanks to the lightning fast abilities of the Internet, the social network mediums and the many boards and blogs where like-minded people gather to chat, ideas spring up daily. People who are enthusiastic about a new acquisition can immediately link up with others with the same interests and a think tank can be formed in minutes. We no longer live where we can only "talk shop" at the occasional range outing, organized shoot or gun show, but almost immediately. Ideas are shared at extreme speed and entrepreneurial builders and tinkerers can get to work right away. For all the faults we can find in the Internet, there are certainly plenty of positive uses we can find as well.

Much slower than the speed of the Internet, our beloved printed gun magazines still play an important part in the ingenuity of shootists. At times they are even very complementary of each another. That is where this story begins.

In the January, 2010 issue (Vol. 13, No. 4) of Small Arms Review magazine we published a very in-depth test of the long out of production Jonathan Arthur Ciener commercial version of the Colt belt-fed prototype AR-15/M16 rifles. Within days of the magazine hitting the newsstand, the websites and blogs started buzzing. This design that has roots going as far back as the 1950s and lived a very short commercial life in the late 1980s into the early 1990s was again "discovered" by many people who may not have been involved in the shooting community at this earlier time. Several questions about its viability today and the perils or pitfalls of manufacturing of a similar rifle started popping up in numerous conversations. Paying close attention to all the chatter was George DeLury and Bill Grieve of Northridge Tool and Machine, soon to be Valkyrie Armament, LLC.

George was one of several people who called shortly after the article was published to say he was working on a similar design with a few upgrades. I told George, like I told the others, that if he got to the point where they started manufacturing a production version for sale, I would be happy to evaluate it for our readers. About 3 months later I received a second call from George that started with "Hey Jeff, it's George. Remember me? I have something you may want to look at." Within a very short amount of time a large box arrived and that was the first time I saw the BSR-MOD-1 belt-fed AR-15.

The Evolution Continues

Upon initial inspection of the BSR-MOD-1 it looks very much like the currently fielded, higher-end M4s given the use of current furniture and accessories. The base rifle is a Colt Law Enforcement Carbine. The front handguard is a Daniel Defense EZ CAR 7.0 rail with a SAW-type carry handle and E-3 upper receiver topped off with YHM 2-position BUIS folding sights. The rear stock is a 7-position collapsible M4S Ace Ltd. with cheek riser. A Hogue pistol grip and side-mounted sling swivel in the front sight round it off.

Looking at the belt feed mechanism of the Valkyrie BSR-MOD-1 from the outside there are several similarities with the earlier rifles we have examined and tested. It is quite similar in the way it is driven by capturing the energy from the bolt carrier on the recoil (reward) stroke and the feed pawls are also similar. It has the ability to feed from a belt or a standard box magazine with removal of the belt-feed mechanism. It is fed with a modified M27 SAW link in a similar manner to the earlier models as well. There are currently 4 patents pending on this system thus far.

While the basic function seems to mimic the earlier system there are several subtle differences upon closer examination. A favorite design difference of this writer is the addition of a bolt release that protrudes through the feed system. It is a "V" shaped, serrated arm that toggles the bolt release to either hold the bolt back or release it, keeping the shooters fingers far from the feed mechanism. (For those who did not see the test of the Ciener belt-fed rifle, the author ended up with his thumb caught in this extremely tight space during a moment of severe judgment lapse). Another difference is in the belt drive mechanism where the linkage connects to the bolt carrier. Where the original was a fixed pin, the Valkyrie is a removable pin allowing the shooter to completely remove the drive unit when the gun is used with standard box magazines or drums. This serves two purposes. First, the shooter no longer has a reciprocating shuttle in the exterior drive unit when the magazine is being fired. The second benefit is that by removing the link-pin and drive unit, a standard bolt carrier can be used for box magazines including subcaliber units, which was not an option in the earlier versions. Of course the shooter can simply remove the belt-feed unit and be firing from a standard box magazine with the installed bolt carrier in less than a minute without removing the drive pin as well. There are also several other machining differences used in the process of manufacturing that may not have been available 25-50 years ago when the original units were designed.

One major upgrade on the Valkyrie Armament system is the addition of the "V-shaped" serrated lever (A) that engages the bolt hold open lever safely keeping the hands of the user away from the reciprocating mechanism. Another difference is the ability to remove the drive pin (B) allowing the use of a standard, unmodified bolt carrier for subcaliber units when the belt feed mechanism is removed and the mag well is stylized for feeding.

In the area of feeding, a downfall of this system has always been the lack of excess and residual energy to capture and assist in pulling the belt into the mechanism. This necessitated a belt box so the length of pull was kept short. Colt designed (and Ciener later utilized) a very nice box that pinned on the bottom of the rifle and doubled as a link chute, which captured the expended links and stored them in a separate compartment for reuse. The Valkyrie BSR-MOD-1 uses an adapter for standard NATO SAW boxes. While the Ciener feed box is very nice and even doubles as a link catcher as a big advantage, SAW Boxes are readily available and multiple boxes can be preloaded and stored or taken out at the same time. We like both designs for their individual advantages. Valkyrie Armament will be releasing a detachable link chute and box in the very near future but it was not available for testing at the time this went to print. We understand it is made of Kydex and will hold 200 links.

Serious Business

While Valkyrie Armament's key market is geared towards recreational shooters at the current time, it isn't being built as a "one off" or custom order only project. Even though they are pleased to convert your own gun to utilize their belt-feed system, they are manufacturing and stocking complete rifles of numerous configurations for immediate shipment. Spare parts are all on hand and are available for purchase. Custom builds certainly are available, such as conversions on registered M16s, piston-type rifles and they even manufacture a special line for the MGI Hydra MARCK-15 system taking full advantage of the quick change barrel (QCB) system. To date they have even converted a water-cooled M16; so if you think your project is "outside the box" please don't discard it without calling them first. While Colt manufactured rifles are preferred for conversions due to their consistent tolerances, they have not found any rifles they could not convert at the time of this writing. Some that take longer, requiring additional custom fitting may incur additional fees and Valkyrie Armament is happy to quote special jobs on request.

Range Time & Operation

The rifle was an instant hit out of the box, but the proof is always in the performance and not the looks. Since this writer is very familiar with these types of belt systems it was found to be very easy to operate. The rifle comes with a starter tab and an end tab to be linked to each belt. Additional tabs are available for purchase as well as extra links. As mentioned before, the links are a modified, slotted M27 SAW link so factory belted 5.56x45mm ammo will not run in the gun as is. It must be linked with the special links available from Valkyrie Armament, LLC. The current price at this writing is $35 per 100 and they are certainly reusable like any other link.

Rather than go into great length and spend several pages explaining the operating system, since it is so similar to that of the early ArmaLite/Colt/Ciener systems, this writer would urge you to pick up a copy of Vol. 13, No. 4 (January, 2010) issue of Small Arms Review for extremely detailed information about the operation and feed system. (If they become difficult to obtain we will make every effort to post a PDF of the article on the Small Arms Review website in the near future.)

The shooting debut of this system for our initial function testing was at a large invitational machine gun shoot held at the Williams Machine Gun Range in North Anson, Maine. Since we are very familiar with Murphy's Law we knew if we made a big announcement that we had one to test it would be destined to not function properly. It was concealed as well as it could be until the first few belts, but we were sniffed out and a small crowd had gathered to watch even though the majority of the firing line had no idea what we were doing. Since all we needed to do this day was determine if it functioned properly we loaded several small belts and were very pleased it ran them without a hitch.

The BSR-MOD-1 functioned with belts and magazines equally well, even in very cold conditions.

Further firing was conducted (and continues as of this writing) at the Small Arms Research Test Range in central Maine. The bulk of the testing has been function testing and it has allowed several other tests to run concurrent. We wanted to see if the extra duty the bolt carrier needed to perform had any effect on the accuracy and found no difference in either group size or point of impact when switching between the box magazine and the belt. Since the ejection was very positive and consistent we decided to conduct a belt pull test. The early guns are known for a weakness in this area so we had limited expectations. We started with a short length of 20 rounds and kept adding 7 rounds after firing 2 rounds to give us a 5 round net addition each time until we found the point it would no longer pull a hanging belt with reliability. This system didn't prove to last but a few cycles when we switched to adding ammo in 50-round lengths. We started the new protocol at 50 rounds and fired 3 rounds. This continued to 100 rounds, 150 rounds and 200 rounds. The length of the belt was so long that we needed to utilize a ladder to keep it from dragging on the ground. At 200 rounds we found it would not function reliably. It would fire 2 or 3 and stop. We cut back to 150 rounds and found the same result. 3 or 4 or 5 rounds and it would stop. At this point we started removing 25 rounds instead of 50 and continued testing with a 125-round belt. The result was the end of the belt pull testing as it easily cycled through the remainder of the hanging belt with ease. Remembering we were shooting a dry gun around the 100 round mark we stopped long enough to lightly lubricate the bolt carrier where it interfaces with the drive pin and continued to empty the belt. Since we were evaluating a semiautomatic this time we couldn't take belt whip into consideration, which can create additional forces under fully automatic fire. We found the number of rounds it would fire from a hanging belt was an amazing 125 rounds, which was far more than the original designs would reliably handle. The weight of 125 belted rounds, using 55gr Federal XM-193 ammo was approximately 3.75 pounds. Considering the length of pull is only between 8 rounds and 20 rounds when using a standard SAW box (depending on the number of rounds in the box), and the hanging weight of that belt is between 3.9 ounces and 9.6 ounces, having the ability to feed and function reliably with approximately 600% of the normal feed forces, we found to be a huge reliability margin.

The "Up-Tight" Saw Box was designed by Thomas Cassidy and marketed by Valkyrie Armament, LLC. It is a modified belt box designed to hold higher on the gun and attach to the original Valkyrie belt-feed unit. We found them very well made and quite useful. Since the mechanism must be mounted inside the box it will reduce the capacity slightly. We found 170 rounds would still fit comfortably with the possibility for a few more.

Conclusions

The Valkyrie Armament, LLC BSR-MOD-1 was a hit, right out of the box. It was meticulously manufactured and the fit and finish matched the host gun very well. It looked like it could have been completely manufactured by Colt given the strait, clean receiver cuts and feed mechanism. It was a perfect match to the host firearm. The function was everything we had hoped it would be, not failing in any form of feeding, firing and ejecting except for when we purposely overloaded the weight of the belt for the hanging belt test to find the point of failure. It is fun to shoot and when compared to similar firearms, although this one is quite unique in its availability as a modification to your own host firearm the price seemed like a bargain for a modern belt-fed. At the time of this writing the retail pricing for a conversion on your host gun is $3,300 with approximately a 3-week turnaround time. Since it has an 85% parts compatibility with any regular AR-15 type firearm, parts are readily available and even specific parts to this conversion are in stock and available from Valkyrie Armament,

LLC. If you are a Black Rifle aficionado and need a new model to kindle the fire, we think you will enjoy this conversion. If you live in an area where you can't own machine guns, a belt-fed semiautomatic AR-15 rifle is pretty high on the fun meter. For those with lightning links and registered Drop In Auto Sears, yes, this will run fine as long as you get the proper bolt carrier.

At $35 per 100 links at the current time, it is expected that this price will go down as they continue to increase the quantity of links they manufacture. Make sure you police your links and it will keep the cost of shooting way down. If only it used a standard link...

But Wait, There's More!

As we are going to press we have been notified that several variants are being tested with standard M27 SAW links. This is an exciting development and definitely raises the bar on the usefulness of the system and the cost of operation. Not only are standard links very inexpensive, it can be purchased already linked. The best part has yet to be told though - if you have one of the current models (MOD-1) you will receive the "Standard Link Upgrade" (MOD-2) for free so you don't have to stand on the sidelines and wait for the latest gun in fear of the next generation passing you over. And just in case the whole "Belt-Fed .223" concept doesn't catch your attention, we thought we would mention the .308 AR-10 prototype being tested and prepped for production and release in early 2012.

Shrike 5.56 Advanced Weapons System

The author fires a Shrike on an M-16 M4 during some desert testing.

For several years there have been underground rumblings concerning something called "The Shrike" that was going to change the way we look at and utilize the M16 series. That day has finally arrived. Manufactured by Ares Defense Systems, it is poised to hit the market in late February and it has been one of the most anticipated weapons systems in recent memory.

The Shrike 5.56(tm) is a "drop on" belt-feed upper receiver assembly for the AR-15/M16 family of firearms. It requires absolutely no permanent modification to the lower receiver and allows the shooter the option of belt feed operation while still allowing the alternate use of the standard M16 detachable box-type magazine at the operator's discretion. This new upper receiver assembly is an accessory and not a firearm in and of itself.

The namesake of this revolutionary new unit is oddly enough, a bird. The Northern Shrike (Lanius excubitor), native to Canada is sometimes referred to as the butcherbird because of its practice of impaling its prey on thorns and barbed wire similar to the way butcher hangs meat in their shops. It is a small creature that packs an enormous amount of power, which also seems to describe this new weapons system perfectly.

The Shrike was invented and designed by Geoffrey A. Herring of Ares Defense Systems in Blackburg, Virginia. It was originally conceived by Herring as a way to provide the rifle squad with a Squad Automatic Weapon (SAW) without subtracting a rifleman. In order to meet this MENS (Mission Essential Need Statement) strict design parameters were required.

The weight was a major concern and with the complete rifle in the M4 configuration, including the Shrike unit, weighing in at less than 8 pounds, empty, Herring was well under the average 15-27-pound guns that troops were currently fielding.

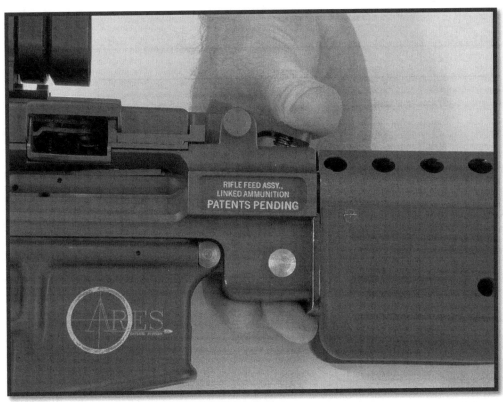

To remove the barrel, this lever is depressed with the thumb and the barrel can slide straight out and separate from the gas system.

As the M16 has been our primary service weapon for over 40 years, as well as that of many of our major allies, it seemed to be a natural choice as the host firearm for the Shrike. There were several attractive aspects to this, i.e., a substantial number of trained service personal already familiar with the M16 lower receiver, as well as a large national inventory already of spare parts necessary for the lower half of the firearm. This presented a cost-effective concept for the potential users

The Shrike, well suited for military and law enforcement applications, was also designed to be a user-friendly system for civilian shooters and class III enthusiasts also. The system was developed with the idea that it must be able to function in a semiautomatic-only variation that would be adaptable to the thousands of AR-15 rifles in private hands. This brings a whole new dimension of shooting to those who do not live in class III friendly states, have trouble with their "Cleo's" signing off on BATF Form

67

4s or just don't want to spend the money or engage in the hassle of lengthy paperwork required to buy a registered machine gun.

Shrike on display at SAR Show 2002 in Phoenix.

Recreational and competitive shooters will love the option to use belts rather than standard box magazines for several reasons. Box magazines are easily damaged, cumbersome while trying to shoot from the prone position and they are becoming more expensive every day. The M27 links used with the Shrike are currently inexpensive and plentiful and when the box magazine is not inserted, the weapon can be much lower to the ground or shooting bench. For those who have purchased their AR-15 since 1994 and have guns considered to be "post-ban," Ares Defense is offering a Shrike in a post-ban configuration.

Class III enthusiasts certainly have something to celebrate with the introduction of the Shrike. Since the 1986 ban on machine gun manufacture for civilian ownership has gone into effect, prices on transferable guns have gone through the roof. There were very few belt-fed machine guns chambered in 5.56x45mm NATO prior to the ban and prices on the ones that were available have become out of reach for most collectors. Before the introduction of the Shrike the only options were to spend in excess of $40,000 on a transferable Stoner 63(A) when one was available, or if you were fortunate enough to have a Class III license you could have purchased a "Pre-86" dealers sample FN Minimi in the area of $60,000 - $70,000 or more. Now we have the option of purchasing an M16 in the area of

$6,000, adding a Shrike for another $2,995 and having a 5.56x45mm NATO belt-fed machine gun for well under $10,000.

The Shrike functions with either readily available M27 ammunition links or with the standard M16 box magazine currently on the market. Unlike the Stoner 63 there is no need to rearrange any parts when swapping from one feed type to the other. You can fire a magazine and empty it, lift the top cover and drop a belt into the feed tray, hit the bolt release to chamber a round and fire the belt until it is gone. Once the belt is gone you can insert another box magazine into the magazine-well, charge the firearm and continue firing.

The receiver of the Shrike is manufactured from 7075-T6 forgings. The quick-change barrel includes a barrel extension with non-adjustable headspace. It is gas-piston-operated and the standard hand-guard is insulated with a sheet-metal heat shield. Most of the parts are proprietary. Early prototypes used M16 bolts but Ares found that manufacturing their own parts, with their own modified design specifications results in a better end product. As it stands now, the only part that is unmodified from a standard M16 upper receiver assembly is the firing pin.

The lower receiver remains unmodified with the exception of adding a stronger main spring to assist in stripping rounds from the links, which require a higher stripping force than from a standard box magazine. The bolt catch supplied with the Shrike is also different, as the top section is displaced slightly rearward to bring it out from behind the feed tray. This part exchange takes less than three minutes and does not affect the way your lower receiver operates with any standard upper receiver.

Most weapons share several functions with existing weapons and the Shrike is no exception. Early pioneers in the art of gun design such as John Browning, Sir Hiram Maxim and Melvin Johnson developed principals that continue to be utilized and improved upon and new designers employ these principals along with new ideas to achieve their products. The Shrike uses a two-step shuttle feed with a traditional top cover such as the MG42. The quick-change barrel system is similar to that of the Stoner 63(A). Unique features not found in other weapons systems include mating of the Shrike to the factory lower receiver exactly like the original upper receiver and providing the option of using belts or magazines without modifying the lower receiver.

The fire control is exactly the same as your standard AR-15 or M16 and is not changed in any way by the addition of the Shrike upper receiver. If you have a semiautomatic-only AR-15, it will function in "SAFE-SEMI" just like the original. Since the bottom of Shrike bolt carrier was designed to provide the same functions as the original bolt carrier in the factory upper receiver, if you purchase the semiautomatic-only version, it will function with a registered lightning link. If you have burst fire control components in your lower receiver you will achieve the same performance with the Shrike upper as you do with the factory upper receiver, thus providing a closed-bolt "SAFE-SEMI-BURST" function. If you have a four-position trigger mechanism you will still be provided with a closed-bolt "SAFE-SEMI-BURST-FULL" function. If you have an open-bolt fire control mechanism such as the unit designed by Henry Tatro of Colt Industries, you will have an open-bolt "SAFE-FULL" mechanism such as the one used in the Colt M16A2 LMG, Model 750. A standard M16 type Shrike bolt carrier will have to be modified to work in this system and Ares Defense may provide this service to their customers at some point in the future.

The TAC(tm) trigger system invented by Terry Soper produces a closed-bolt "SAFE-SEMI-SEMI/AUTO" function very similar to the Steyr AUG rifle. When the "AUTO" position is selected the operator can fire in either "SEMI" or "FULL" depending upon the amount of force applied to the trigger. All of the above trigger mechanisms will function and may be used with Shrike as described.

Ares Defense has designed a few of their own trigger systems to work with their upper receiver to permit open-bolt fire in the "FULL" position when installed in a registered lower receiver. Because the Bureau of Alcohol, Tobacco and Firearms (BATF) has ruled that an open-bolt firing mechanism installed in a semiautomatic-only firearm manufactured after 1981 would be a machine gun in and of itself, they designed these only to fit registered MIL-spec lower receivers. The first variation produces an open-bolt "SAFE-AUTO" function. The second variation produces a closed-bolt "SAFE-SEMI" and an open-bolt "AUTO" function. These will both be available as accessory options for those with approved Form 4's or an FFL/SOT.

When I inquired as to what configurations the Shrike would be offered in, Geoff smiled and quoted Henry Ford's famous "You can have any color Ford that you want, but they will all leave the factory black." He said that in order to keep cost to a minimum for the end users they have settled on one basic configuration that should fit the majority of applications. A standard unit will be shipped with a 16-inch non-chrome-lined quick-change barrel with a twist rate of one turn in 9 inches. It will have a nylon-insulated handguard, fixed sights, and a MIL-STD-1913 rail on the top cover, and a 1/4-inch small front take down pin. An offset pin can be used to mate it to the large-hole Colt AR-15s. Purchasers will have the option of a full-auto or semiautomatic-only bolt carrier and a pre-ban or post-ban barrel. The only difference between the full-auto and the semiautomatic-only is the stripped bolt carrier. The post-ban barrel has no threads and employs a permanently attached muzzle brake as per BATF guidelines and the pre-ban barrel has a standard 1/2x28 thread with a flash hider.

There are several accessories that will be available for the Shrike. Some are shorter barrels (13 - 20 inches), bipods, tactical barrel bags, SAW belt-box adapters, tripod T&E adapters, folding sights, a belt-linking machine and more. Proof of approved Form 4 or FFL/SOT must accompany any order for barrels shorter than 16 inches or for any open-bolt fire control components.

Just like any firearm, barrel life is going to depend heavily on maintenance and type of usage. If the operator practices good fire control discipline and regularly maintains the system the barrel should meet or exceed 20,000 rounds. If the shooter fires in 200-round bursts, reloads and does it over and over, (like we often see at large recreational events) barrel life will be significantly shorter.

Offering the Shrike in other calibers is not something on the horizon at this time. Many people have expressed interest in a 7.62x39mm caliber but it doesn't seem practical now. The only belts that are really available for this caliber are Soviet RPD belts and Czech VZ-52 belts, both being fairly rare and somewhat expensive. The fact that they are both of a non-disintegrating design will further hinder performance of the Shrike due to the link ejection port being positioned above the brass ejection port. Just like there is an exception to every rule, there may be potential for one more caliber though. Where some countries do not allow civilian ownership of firearms in calibers slated for military use, the 5.56x45mm NATO may be restricted in some areas. If there were enough demand, Ares Defense would not rule out a conversion for .222 Remington that could be accomplished with a simple barrel change.

Shooting the Shrike

Photos from the "belt pull test." 100-round hanging belts were used during regular firing. We tested the limits of the Shrike by trying 200-round and 300+ round belts and eventually ran out of height when we had the gun over 10' from the ground and it continued to feed without difficulty.

The configuration we brought to the range was a pre-production model with a 14-inch barrel in M4 configuration. We opted to use an optional vertical pistol grip on the front handguard. Before we started shooting we all had a briefing on the Shrike System and it was explained that we were shooting the last experimental, pre-production model manufactured before final production was implemented. Herring made us aware of upgrades implemented between manufacturing this model and the production model that would be shipped very soon. The level of research and development that had gone into this project over the last few years was now becoming obvious, as no detail seemed to be left to chance.

As we began the testing, Herring demonstrated the ability of the lower receiver, now with the Shrike upgrade of the new spring and bolt catch installed, to operate flawlessly with a M4A1 "standard issue" upper receiver as used by USSOCOM forces. He inserted a 30-round magazine and emptied it immediately. After the magazine was empty the bolt was locked open by the magazine follower such as in any standard AR15/M16. Now it was time to get to the Shrike.

The first of our tasks was to test the Shrike for belt pull. Many people who are not familiar with a belt feed mechanism are not aware of the amount of energy necessary to operate the action. It takes much more energy to strip a round from a belt than it does to strip a round from a conventional box magazine. In a box magazine the rounds are usually under spring tension being forced in the direction of the action and will automatically advance as each round is fired. In a Belt feed mechanism the action of the firearm must actually pull the belt into the mechanism and this requires additional energy. When you add the additional weight of an extremely long and heavy belt the extra energy necessary required to run the action is compounded.

Herring was first to shoot the Shrike in this testing phase and had actually been shooting 100-round hanging belts since this project was in its early stages. This was something he did on a regular basis and once again this task was accomplished with ease. After a brief conversation he loaded a hanging 200-round belt from the Shrike and held it over his head to try and keep the belt from hitting on the ground. A few rounds were fired in "SEMI" and then he switched the selector to "AUTO" and emptied the remainder of the belt without a malfunction. Everyone was satisfied with these results as it was an extreme situation because the belt is usually only pulled from a very short distance, most typically a hanging ammo box that is mounted immediately below the receiver. Since we were conducting a test we decided to push on. A belt over 300 rounds was linked and Herring had to stand on the tailgate of one of our test vehicles and hold the gun high over his head again to get as many rounds in the air as possible. At this point there was over 10 feet of linked 5.56x45mm NATO ammunition hanging from the feed tray of the Shrike. He again fired a couple of rounds on "SEMI" and switched the selector to "FULL." After firing approximately thirty to forty rounds feeding flawlessly in "FULL," he switched it back to "SAFE" and jumped down off the tailgate. Everyone in attendance decided that if this portion of the test were to go any further we would need an extremely long ladder. Our collective feeling was that it passed the belt pull test with flying colors and I even think it exceeded Herring's own expectations.

The second phase of testing was to swap the feed device from one method of feed to another and back again without changing or altering the configuration, or even cleaning out remaining links from the link chute of the feed tray. We wanted to find out how it would function in a situation where a belt was expended and the availability of more ammo was only a standard 30-round box magazine. And then going one step further, load with another belt.

A belt was loaded into the Shrike and it was charged. The entire belt was emptied and the bolt chugged forward. Upon this happening a loaded magazine was loaded into the factory magazine well and the charging handle was pulled back and dropped home. The entire 30 rounds were emptied in a few short bursts. With this, the magazine release was hit and the magazine fell to the ground. The top cover was lifted, another belt was inserted and with one hit of the bolt release, a round was stripped from the belt and locked into battery for firing. A few short bursts later and the last of the linked ammo was swallowed up by the Shrike. This test was also performed without failure.

Our next phase was to get the unit in the hands of several testers and get everyone's individual opinion of comfort and controllability. All opted for a large belt and had different types of trigger discipline. Some fired several short bursts, some fired a small burst and a large burst and some just dumped their belts. Some of the shooters mentioned the presence of a slight "trigger-slap" and others felt nothing different than a standard M16 at all. The consensus of all the shooters, regardless of shooting style, was that the gun was very controllable and comfortable to shoot.

In absolute fairness, as the Shrike System definitely exceeded our expectations overall, the day was not without a few predictable slow-downs. As mentioned above, there were a couple of upgrades Herring implemented between this last pre-production model and those being manufactured for sale. One of these production upgrades consisted of changing the pin that secures the non-reciprocating charging handle to the bolt for cocking. On the early prototype the pin was simply pressed in and had a tendency to want to walk out. The production model has this pin cross-drilled and pinned to the charging handle to completely alleviate this problem. We experienced one slowdown due to this pin walking out as expected.

The second slowdown we experienced occurred when the pin that is part of the operating rod assembly sheared. Even with a problem of this magnitude, amazingly enough the system still continued to function firing in a three-shot burst mode. This problem has already been addressed as well in the series production phase by simply instituting an engineering change notice. All of our concerns were addressed and corrected prior to the first production run and we are now anxiously awaiting of the first shipment of the Shrike .556 Advanced Weapons System to arrive to their new owners.

Watch the pages of Small Arms Review for a future "Torture Test" and detailed photographic field strip and disassembly of the Shrike and information on new upgrades and accessories including the adaptation of the modified M203 40mm Grenade Launcher.

About the Ares Defense System

Ares Defense Systems is an acronym for Advanced Research and Engineering Services for Defense Systems. Geoffrey A. Herring formed and licensed the company with BATF in 1997, in an effort to transform his passion for designing firearms and mechanisms into a business. Small arms study and metal machining have been cornerstones of Herring's life since childhood.

Ares Defense Systems, LLC is primarily a Research & Development Laboratory with manufacturing capabilities. While some production components are sub-contracted to other establishments, the major portion of the products are machined in-house on MAZAK vertical and horizontal CNC machining centers. In addition to their own in-house projects, Ares Defense Systems, LLC provides small arms consultation and if needed, prototype development for companies with new and innovative small arms products.

Ares Defense Shrike 5.56 Advanced Weapons System

Caliber:	5.56x45 mm NATO
Overall Length:	742 mm (29.25 inches) with a 14.25" barrel and telescoping stock
Barrel Length:	330 mm (13") through 508mm (20")
Weight, with full mag:	6.35 kg (14 pounds) with 200-round loaded SAW box
Weight, Empty:	3.62 kg (8 pounds)
Weight of full mag:	.445 kg (1 pound for 30-round magazine) 2.26 kg (5 pounds for 200-round SAW box)
Number of Barrel grooves:	Six-Groove
Twist of Rifling:	Right Hand
Pitch of Rifling:	1/228 mm (1/9" std. non-chrome lined for commercial; 1/175 mm(1/7 inches std. chrome lined for military L/E)
Muzzle Velocity:	899mps (2,950 fps) for 14.25", 990mps 3,250 fps for 20"
Firing Modes:	SAFE-SEMI (closed bolt), SAFE-SEMI-AUTO (closed bolt), AUTO (open bolt)
Rate of Fire:	625 RPM
Method of Operation:	Gas piston, short stroke, tappet
Lockup Method:	Rotating multi-lug bolt and barrel extension
Finish on Metal Surfaces:	Aluminum parts are Hard-Coat Anodized per MIL-A-8625, Type III Class 2. Steel parts are Phosphate finished per MIL-STD-171.
Construction of Receiver:	Forged and machined, 7075-T6 Aluminum Alloy
Furniture:	Polymer forearm is standard, M1913 Picatinny Rail type forearm as an option
Optical Sight:	M1913 Picatinny Rail on top cover provides for mounting of optics and NVDs
Front Sight:	Protected post
Rear Sight:	Protected peep
Sight Radius	419 mm 16.5" for all models

STAG-15L: The Sinistral Semi-automatic from Stag Arms

If there has ever been a group of people who were truly disadvantaged on the shooting range, it has been the southpaws. From bolt-action rifles to belt-fed machine guns, firearms have historically been designed around the framework of the right-handed end user. Given the typical ejection path of most semiautomatic and fully automatic firearms, many people who shoot left-handed are quite "gun-shy" when handling these guns for the first time with brass ejecting through (or extremely close to) their line of sight. Thanks to Stag Arms of New Britain Connecticut, left-handed fans of the Black Rifle can consider this problem a thing of the past.

Stag Arms, LLC was founded in May of 2003, but their experience in manufacturing AR-15 and M16 type rifles and parts goes back more than 30 years. An offshoot of their sister company, Continental Manufacturing, all the major components of the Stag Arms line of rifles are manufactured "in house." None of the components utilized in the Stag Arms rifles are imported or manufactured outside the United States.

The original concept of the left-handed AR-15 type rifle actually started even before the formation of the company- in fact there have been some attempts at this in the past. The Stag Arms left handed AR-15 story starts in 1998, when some of the initial manufacturing parts were ordered in anticipation of the project. 5 years later when Stag Arms was founded by Mark Malkowski, the project was re-started and the rest of the necessary development continued. Since the original concept rifle, the STAG-15L has become a completely new upper receiver system, compatible with any original lower receiver.

There is much more work necessary than reversing a few off the shelf parts in order to manufacture and assemble the STAG-15L. The bolt and bolt carrier needed to be completely redesigned and all of the coinciding features of the upper receiver itself had to be redesigned to match these new internal changes. In order to eject from the left side of the rifle the ejection port must be relocated from the right side to the left. This would involve a complete redesign of the upper receiver including the relocation of the dust cover, brass deflector and forward assist assembly. Due to the location of the bolt-hold-open feature on the lower receiver, the dust cover must now open up towards the carry handle instead of opening down towards the magazine well. This way the bolt-hold-open lever operates as intended and is unobstructed.

As soon as the bolt carrier is removed from the rifle many of the internal changes become apparent. The most obvious change is the addition of the notches on the left side of the bolt to be used in conjunction with the newly designed forward assist assembly. The right side of the bolt is smooth and is not notched. At the front of the bolt carrier, the gas relief ports are on the left side to coincide with the location of the new ejection port. In addition, the slot the bolt cam-pin rides in is also reversed and the cam pin must be removed to the right of the carrier key during disassembly. The firing pin retaining pin must also be removed from the right side of the carrier to disassemble the carrier and remove the firing pin and bolt. The carrier key is no different than the key in a standard bolt carrier.

Removing the bolt will reveal a few more major changes. The bolt cam pinhole in an AR-15/M16 bolt is undersized on one side so that the bolt may only be able to be installed in the bolt carrier in one position. On a standard bolt carrier when the bolt is installed and fully extended to the ejection position, looking at the face of the bolt, the extractor is in the 10 o'clock position. On the STAG-15L bolt, during the same function, the extractor is in the 2 o'clock position. The undersized side of the bolt cam pinhole in the STAG-15L is reversed to accommodate this change. The user should be cautioned to be extremely careful not to mix up right handed and left handed bolts during assembly as it is possible for these two parts to be interchanged even though they will not function properly and cause serious problems. A quick check as to the position of the extractor will allow the user to be certain the correct bolt is in place. The bolt carrier is clearly marked "Left-Handed" on the right rear side and a similar marking on these special bolts could be a worthy upgrade in the future to help avoid potential confusion with new AR-15 style rifle owners.

The firing pin, bolt cam pin, firing pin retaining pin, ejector, extractor, and bolt gas rings are standard factory parts.

The STAG-15L sent to SAR for evaluation was their Model 1L. In this configuration the rifle has a 16-inch, M4 contoured barrel and 6-position collapsible stock. The upper receiver, though left handed, was of an A3 configuration employing the use of a detachable carry handle with a fixed front sight. All the STAG-15 guns have a 1/9 twist rate and are chrome lined. Also available are the following models:

- **Model 2L** - 16-inch, M4 contoured barrel and 6-position collapsible stock. No carry handle and utilized an A.R.M.S. #40 rear flip-up sight along with the A2 front post.
- **Model 3L** - 16-inch, M4 contoured barrel and 6-position collapsible stock. No sights, only M1913 Picatiny Rail flat top upper receiver and M1913 Picatiny Rail front sight platform.
- **Model 4L** - 20-inch barrel with A2 buttstock and detachable carry handle and front sight post.
- **Models 1, 2, 3 & 4** (no letter "L" suffix) are also available from Stag Arms in the same configuration as those listed above, in a traditional right-hand design.

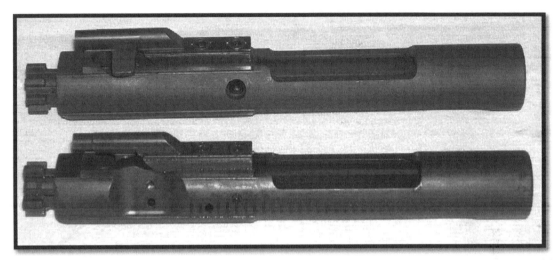

A standard AR-15 bolt and carrier assembly above a left-handed Stag-15L bolt and carrier assembly. The Stag-15L group had to be drastically modified to eject from the left and all major components are completely different.

Stag Arms offers these complete rifles and all have an ambidextrous safety selector on the lower receiver making them even more comfortable to the left-handed user. Another accessory offered through Stag Arms for their STAG-15L series of rifles is the Norgon Ambi-Catch. This accessory replaces the standard magazine release and allows the user to release the magazine on the left side of the receiver by rotating this new latch without changing the function of the magazine release button on the right side of the receiver. Upper receiver assemblies can be purchased separately for those who already have a lower receiver and full-auto compatible bolt carriers can also be purchased for owners of registered receivers and drop-in auto sears.

Shooting the STAG-15L made this right-handed shooter aware of, and appreciate the importance of, the brass deflector. The brass pile was growing to the left rear side of the shooter dropping at approximately the 8 o'clock position. One quick glance at the deflector, suddenly colored with fresh brass strikes, made me realize what a great innovation that was for the left-handed M16 shooters of days past. It was thoughtful of Stag Arms to include this feature for right-handed shooters who want to utilize their left-handed rifle.

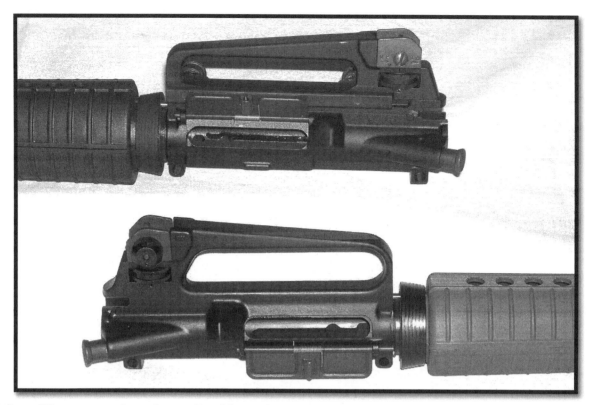

A Stag-15L upper receiver above a Doublestar Star-15 upper receiver. In order for the operator to properly utilize the bolt hold open feature, the dust cover has to flip up instead of down when placed on the left side of the rifle.

To stay with the program, several magazines were fired from the left shoulder and practice using the left eye. With a little concentration it was actually more comfortable than I thought possible. The difference was that it was not instinctual and fast, but a slow process that actually required concentration during every step. Knowing how disadvantaged it is to be forced to fire from the opposite shoulder and eye, I can now fully understand how exciting a project the STAG-15L actually is for many members of our shooting community.

Summary

The quality of the STAG-15L is excellent. The markings on the STAG line of rifles are deep and clean and the logo is distinctive and attractive. The fit and finish is very nice and the rifle submitted for evaluation never malfunctioned under any circumstance. We even tested it in sub-freezing temperatures with the new NATEC Polymer Cased Ammunition (see accompanying article in this issue of Small Arms Review) and it never skipped a beat. During most of the shooting time, we were using Wolf 62-grain FMJ and Norinco 55-grain FMJ ammunition. The 1 in 9 inch twist barrel seemed to accommodate both rounds with ease, and at distances of 50 yards and 100 yards, all met their intended marks in a series of B27 Silhouette targets.

Shooters who have had the opportunity to handle the STAG-15L has been very intrigued. Those intimately familiar with the AR-15/M16 family of weapons have especially taken interest in the redesign of the parts necessary to accomplish the proper extraction and ejection. The few southpaws who have seen it have been ecstatic. I would recommend the STAG-15L to any left-handed shooter who wants to feel like they finally have an instrument made for them. I would also recommend it to any collector of the AR-15/M16 family of firearms who is looking for an interesting "gap" to fill in their collection, even if they didn't realize it previously existed.

Specifications STAG-15L	
Model:	1L
Caliber:	5.56x.45 NATO
Overall Length:	32 inches (812.8 mm) stock collapsed
Barrel Length:	16 inches (406.4 mm)
Number of Grooves:	6 – chrome lined
Rifling Twist & Pitch:	Right hand, 1/9 inches (1/228 mm)
Rear Sight:	Detachable carry handle w/A2 adjustable
Front Sight:	Protected post
Weight, Empty:	6.75 pounds (3.06 kg)
Weight of Full Magazine:	1 pound (.445 kg)
Magazine Capacity:	30-round magazine
Selector / Safety:	Ambidextrous
Stock:	6-position collapsible
MSRP as Tested:	$989.00

The POF P-416 Weapons System

POF 9.25-inch system

At the Arizona State Fairgrounds during the SAR Show in 2003, Frank Desomma of Patriot Ordnance Factory (POF) showed an early prototype of what would eventually become the P-416 Weapons System; billed as the future of M16 weapons systems. He continued to work and refine his new system, and in early 2006 he sent SAR two semiautomatic production models for evaluation: one with a 9.25 inch barrel and the other with a 16-inch barrel.

The POF P-416 with C.R.O.S. (Corrosion Resistant Operating System) is an op-rod and gas piston driven M16 weapons system enhancement. It has completely eliminated the traditional gas tube and the unpopular issues associated with it. It has been stated many times that the greatest flaw of the M16 family of firearms may be that it forces gas and debris into the receiver via the gas tube, directly above the magazine. This is effectively dumping the waste in the same area the feeding takes place. The P-416 appears to completely address this design feature by capturing everything in the area of the gas block and not allowing residual debris to transfer into the feed mechanism.

In a standard M16, as the bullet passes the gas block (doubling as the front sight), residual gasses are channeled into the gas port. The gasses are transferred through the gas tube into the bolt carrier through the bolt key. The pressure created by these gasses causes the rearward travel of the bolt carrier, unlocking the bolt and ejecting the fired case. With this transfer of gas, necessary for this system to function, comes other undesirable variables including unburned propellant debris and heat. With a brief look inside the operating mechanism after firing several magazines, the residual debris quickly become apparent. The extra heat transferred through the gas tube may be immediately noticeable with heavy sustained fire or may take a long time to create potential problems culminating with gas tube malfunctions ranging from gas port erosion problems to simple excessive use malfunctions.

The P-416 operates like a standard M16 in that the gas behind the exiting bullet is directed through a port into the gas block, but that is where the similarities in the gas system end. In the P-416, the gasses contact a piston just behind the gas block and cause it to travel to the rear. The gas piston pushes the op-rod which in turn pushes the bolt carrier rearward. Due to the fact that the op-rod is solid, carries no gas and only travels rearward itself, all residual gasses and debris are dissipated in the area of the gas piston, never reaching the receiver area. The inside of the receiver is not coated with flakes of powder and a film of carbon as is commonly the case with standard M16 variants.

Some people believe that the excessive heat transferred through the gas tube during heavy fire can create a potential for serious problems, even if not immediately apparent. With the bolt carrier and bolt reaching high temperatures and cooling over and over, it may create a problem with the strength of the metal causing it to become brittle over time. Due to the piston and op-rod design of the P-416, these concerns are addressed by capturing the residual heat and debris in and around the gas block, and not allowing their transfer back inside the receiver.

A view looking through the EOTech holographic sight and the FTA 2005 front sight. They worked well alone and in combination.

Since the bolt carrier is no longer utilized as a "gas trap" and responsible for the sealing of the moving gasses, the gas rings are removed from the bolt and the gas key was replaced with a special solid key that, on early guns, is bolted into a milled slot in the new carrier. Later bolt carriers in this system are 1-piece units where the "key" is machined out of the same material as the carrier thus forming one single piece. This will further the life of the unit by providing an even stronger impact area for the op-rod and ensuring a strait push rearward to avoid flex problems that were encountered on earlier prototype units. The bolt and carrier of the P-416 are both chrome plated and heat treated to Mil Spec.

The absence of the gas rings on the bolt serves an additional purpose of extremely reducing the amount of friction in the recoil system. The gas rings on a standard M16 bolt and bolt carrier need to create a seal so that the gas pressure is adequate to operate the recoil system. To create this gas seal, there is a necessary metal-to-metal contact that causes the friction. This is no longer necessary with the P-416 system. Upon pulling the charging handle the first few times it is obvious that the system in this aspect is much "looser" than a traditional M16.

POF has taken advantage of this reduced friction property and have compounded it by adding a coating of Silicon Nickel to the inside of the upper receiver and the interior surface of the charging handle. This creates an extremely slippery surface and one that seems quite impenetrable by typical debris such as carbon. It also seems to have a very low wear factor based on the results of our testing with the firearms provided.

Strictly as an endurance test, the 9.25-inch barrel version of the P-416 we were provided with had already fired in excess of 5,000 rounds with no cleaning or lubrication. When we received the gun it was obviously dirty upon the initial inspection. In a telephone discussion with Frank Desomma, he laughed and said that since we were going to test one of his units for endurance, he was confident enough in its abilities that he wanted to send one that had already been used extensively instead of something pretty and off the shelf. When he said how many rounds had already been fired through it, the gun was disassembled for inspection. Though the inside of the receivers were amazingly clean, the amount of built-up carbon inside the Krink-style muzzle brake gave all the evidence needed about the number of rounds that had been fired. All of a sudden the number 5,000 did not seem so high anymore.

As further evidence of the number of rounds already fired, there was no way to remove the gas plug with normal hand and finger pressure due to the carbon buildup around the outside of the plug. The detent could be depressed and rotated to the position necessary to remove it, but it would not budge by pulling it forward. Being assured that no tools would be necessary to take it apart, it was time to start improvising. It was noticed that when the charging handle retracted the bolt carrier and the carrier was allowed to slam home, the op-rod would contact the gas piston which would in turn push on the gas plug. After dropping the bolt carrier in this manner several times, the gas plug was out far enough to get a better grip on it and pull the remainder of the way out. The gas piston and op-rod easily dropped out just by tilting the muzzle down with absolutely no resistance.

This excessive carbon around the gas plug was mentioned to Desomma due to the extreme number of rounds since any type of maintainance had been conducted. Desomma said the lugs of the gas plug will be chromed like the barrel of the plug currently is to reduce friction; but we would certainly find that under normal heavy use, removal would not be a problem. He was correct. No tools were necessary to remove the gas plug at any time and he insisted that the manner we used to remove it would not compromise the system in any way.

The upper receiver was reassembled without cleaning or lubricating of any kind, and the lower receiver we were provided with underwent a little makeover. If we were going to do a true SAR endurance test it would be completed in full auto on the correct lower. A few hours in the shop and a Form 2 later, we were ready to rock and roll.

Given that we had a dirty gun to start with, it was decided to jump right into the shooting phase and do some photography after finishing and cleaning up the parts a little. It was at this time we decided to run several data strings to gather information about cyclic rates, chamber temperatures and muzzle velocities while continuing to severely add to the number of rounds fired. The 9.25-inch barrel seemed to lose around 400 fps when compared to the 16-inch version and a little over 250fps compared to a 14.5-inch variant.

POF 16-inch P-415 Recon System

The chamber area temperatures in the P-416 ran surprisingly low, between 80°-92°F after 20-round and 30-round bursts with little time for cooling in between. The standard M16 gas system averaged between 86°F and 120°F under the same conditions. With temperatures being a primary consideration in the P-416 system, POF has designed a special barrel nut that can be used in conjunction with their Predator Rail System that doubles as a heat sink.

Made completely from 7075 T-6 aluminum, it will provide a larger surface area and utilizes cooling fins. This barrel nut will draw the heat from the chamber area faster than usual, creating a cooler operating temperature. This proprietary barrel nut also serves to provide strength and rigidity to the rail system by increasing the mass of the area where the upper receiver connects with the system.

Rates of fire were measured using 3 different buffers. We used the MGI Military Rate Reducing Buffer, the Enidine AR-restor Hydraulic Recoil Buffer and a standard factory buffer. The 16-inch P-416 ran extremely slow and was very controllable with all buffer systems. The muzzle rise was barely noticeable with the both the MGI and the Enidine buffer and was slow enough to be at the point where you could actually count the shots. The MGI averaged slightly fewer than 550 rounds per minute. The Enidine buffer averaged just over 660 rpm and with a factory buffer it was still averaging only 690 rpm. These numbers were all recorded with a standard A2 Flash hider. With any M16 rifle system, the use of accessories such as silencers and certain muzzle brakes can greatly affect the rate of fire. For comparison, we repeated the tests with a Gemtech M4-02 silencer and the increase in rate of fire due to the extra backpressure averaged 279 rpm. We found that using the Krink-style muzzle brake on the 9.25-inch POF-416 even increased the rate of fire by an average of 50 rpm.

The Gas Piston in the 16-inch variant of the P-416 has a reversible feature allowing the operator to compensate for devices like silencers that typically increase the cyclic rates. In normal operating mode the piston is inserted with the 3-groove end towards the muzzle. When silencers or other gas restricting devices are used, the piston can be reversed and inserted with the 2-groove end towards the muzzle. In our ROF tests we found that this allowed the rate of fire to remain a little slower with these devices. When we tested this gas piston change, the rate of fire we recorded with the 3-groove end to the front and a Vortex flash hider averaged 588 rounds per minute utilizing an MGI Rate Reducing Buffer. When the Gemtech M4-02 silencer was added the rate of fire immediately jumped to 851 rpm.

The Troy Industries flip down rear sights are used on several of the POF weapons systems. They are extremely effective, durable, and easy to use.

This is a difference of 263 rpm. When the gas piston was removed and reversed, the cyclic rate instantly dropped to 781 rpm. Simply reversing the gas piston brought the rate of fire down by 70 rpm to a more comfortable 781 rpm. It is important to be noted that the system will not operate at all with the gas piston in this position with standard flash hiders. When the Gemtech M4-02 silencer was removed and the Vortex flash hider was reinstalled, we could not get the P416 to function for more than 3 rounds without a failure to eject.

The rate of fire in the 9.25-inch system was substantially higher than the 16-inch system with a recorded low ROF of 801 rpm with the MGI buffer and a high of 1,108 with a factory buffer. We did not test any sound suppressors on the 9.25-inch system, as many suppressor manufacturers do not recommend use on barrels so short.

The 9.25-inch P-416 system made several trips to the range during the testing period. It was handed to several shooters who were given a briefing on the operating system and they were invited to shoot it all they wanted. Not surprising, several people took advantage of the opportunity. Since we explained that it was an endurance test as well as a standard T&E, several people fired full, 100-round Beta C-Mags, most in a single burst. We lost count of the exact number of rounds fired due to the massive influx of "extra ammunition" fed through it by other shooters but we recorded almost 4,000 more rounds of assorted ammunition fired from our own supply before the gun finally had a failure to eject and was stripped and cleaned. That brings the total to well over 9,000 rounds without cleaning or lubrication of any kind. A simple brushing of the chamber may have been adequate enough to keep going but we used this time as an occasion to end the endurance phase of the testing. The only malfunction encountered during the testing was a broken hammer pin mistakenly utilized when the author installed the full auto parts after converting the lower receiver to fully automatic. The pin was replaced with the correct one and not a single malfunction was recorded until the final failure to eject where we decided to end the test and clean the gun.

The gun was disassembled and thoroughly cleaned. The chamber area was indeed very dirty and there was a little residue in and around the area of the locking lugs. The inside of the upper receiver just wiped clean with a dry cloth exposing the shiny nickel finish showing no signs of wear. The lower receiver had little debris to clean up; mostly a thin film that looked like it had been subject to a heavy layer of smoke for a long period of time. After it was disassembled, cleaned and photographed, it was reassembled and finally lightly lubricated. Every trip to the range since then, it has again been fired extensively and has yet to malfunction again.

The Krink muzzle brake supplied on the 9.25-inch system was well received by everyone who used it. This particular brake had been described in the past as a flash hider, and that statement could not be further from the truth; at least in this barrel length and caliber combination. It was quieter to the shooter than to those observing and seemed to be fairly effective in reducing recoil but it did nothing to hide the flash. Quite the contrary, this brake seems to enhance the flash and force it forward as it does the sound. A short-barreled 5.56x45mm typically has a large diameter flash signature with an ineffective flash hider or in the absence of one. The flash in this configuration is clearly long and narrow creating quite a spectacle even in bright daylight.

The 9.25-inch system combined with the "Krink" style muzzle brake and any of the rate-reducing buffer systems tested proved to be extremely controllable and effective even under full automatic fire.

The Predator rail system was utilized on both test rifles although not necessary for the P-416 gas piston system. The Predator Rail System is a single unit that acts as an extension of a standard flat top upper receiver. It allows the barrel to remain completely free-floating and under no stress from optics and accessories. It is also completely removable allowing the shooter to access the barrel and the gas system. On the 9.25-inch version we used the P-4X and on the 16-inch version we used the P-12X. Just before going to print we received a newer P-12SX, which has a longer bottom rail. The weight of the P-4X is only .66 pounds while the P-12X weighs only 1.15 pounds. Several variants of the Predator Rail System as well as many of the optional accessories we utilized during this article are available directly from POF. Full technical specifications and pricing is available on their website at www.pof-usa.com.

The Predator Rail System

The P-415 / P-416 firearms and upper receivers are available with the Predator rail system. This unique system is machined from a solid piece of aluminum and provides an excellent platform for mounting optics, grips, lights, bipods and any of numerous other accessories. The barrel remains completely free-floating and the proprietary barrel nut even works as a heat sink to keep chamber and barrel temperatures cooler than with standard upper receivers by drawing heat away from the chamber. To disassemble the Predator Rail System first you must remove the two Allen-head screws located on the sides of the system parallel with the barrel nut. These are located at the 3 o'clock and 9 o'clock positions. (Pred1) Next remove the two Allen-head screws located on the top of the system at the 12 o'clock position directly above the barrel nut. After removing those top screws you will notice there are two more screws UNDER the first ones. The second set of screws are holding the barrel nut spacer in place and must also be removed as well. (Pred3) Remove the Allen-head screw at the top rear of the system immediately above the charging handle. (Pred4) At this point grasp the upper receiver in the forward assist area and slide the Predator rail system to the front. (Pred5). The upper receiver will now be separated from the Predator rail system. (Pred7) Reassemble in the reverse order. You will need to realign the barrel nut spacer (A in Pred6) over the barrel nut (B in Pred6) when you begin.

Summary

POF has created a frontrunner with this system. From the well thought-out gas piston, op-rod and carrier group to the impressive Predator rail system, it is a winner in every aspect. The only suggestion to improve upon the system would be the addition of a small tool to assist in removing the gas plug after heavy use, though this may be rectified by the intended hard chroming the lug area of the gas plug as previously discussed.

The front sight utilized with the 9.25-inch P-416 is another effective design from POF. It is called the FTA (Fast Target Acquisition) 2005 Sight and was well received by all who handled the firearm. It has a "no snag" feature due to the sight post being completely enclosed. The most noticeable benefit during our testing was the speed and effectiveness of the sight and the ability to stay on target even under long bursts of full automatic fire. The post in the center of the circle draws your eye into the center if it starts to stray due to the vibration or normal muzzle rise. An additional benefit to those who would use this system for tactical applications is the hood cannot be mistaken for the sight post under poor lighting, or during the necessity for extremely fast target acquisition. The front sight post stands alone very clearly. The sight is removable if the use of optics without its assistance is desired or it may be used in combination with a zero magnification electronic sight. We found both applications were comfortable and easy.

Since arriving for initial testing, the little 9.25-inch system has been the authors "go to" gun and it looks like that will continue. It is extremely well made, very controllable, looks great and functions even better. With the ability to perform through several thousands of varied brands of ammunition throughout several range conditions and continue to run without a hiccup, it is certainly a winner. Operators who must utilize weapons systems in varied conditions should seriously consider evaluating this system for team use. Their reliability factor can certainly be advantageous for times when maintainance, cleaning and lubrication are considered a luxury.

The compact size of the system gives the user an excellent PDW. With a 9.25-inch barrel and overall length of only 27 inches, it is not much larger than an Uzi SMG with the stock extended, which is only 1-inch shorter. The ballistics of the P-416 combined with availability of dependable high capacity magazines and a sturdy rail system capable of numerous tasks should make this a serious contender in any evaluation.

This test systems inclusion of the Krink" muzzle brake only added to the "fun factor" and for someone who loves to shoot recreationally, that has to play an important role. It has been my experience that any fan of the Black Rifle who has the pleasure to try this system will soon wish to acquire one.

The POF-USA P-416 Heavy Fire Endurance Test

Punishing a Piston Gun - Phase II

The subject of the endurance test after the test was over. Over 1,000 rounds of Wolf .223 63-grain FMJ were fired through the P-416 in continuous, 100-round bursts.

It has been almost a year and a half since the original tests, and a review of the data we collected from those outings created a few additional questions that needed to be answered. We noticed that the running temperatures of the P-416 were consistently lower than those taken during the same circumstances with a direct impingement system. It makes perfect sense that the absence of the gas tube redirecting hot gasses into the action would relate to lower operating temperatures but we wanted to find out exactly how much of a difference it would actually make, especially during abnormally heavy usage. This allowed us to set up and began phase II.

Phase II would be another type of endurance test where large amounts of ammo would be fired, in very long, continuous and uninterrupted bursts, possibly bringing the test rifles to the point of catastrophic failure. Upon reaching the predetermined number of rounds, the temperature of the rifle would be measured in several areas, and the testing would immediately continue, allowing for the residual operating temperatures to continue increasing. No cooling time would be allowed.

Since BETA C-Mags are readily available and have worked well for us in past testing of this type, we decided to use them as the baseline and go with 100-round continuous mag dumps. We determined that the complete test would consist of 1,000 rounds, barring any type of system failure. After continuously firing each 100-round burst, the surface temperature would be measured on the following parts: the bolt face, the chamber area, the gas block and the muzzle brake. The surface temperature of

The gas tube can be seen glowing bright red while three cases are suspended in the air and an almost perfect star-burst leaves the muzzle. This rifle, a standard direct gas impingement version faced the same heavy usage as the P-416 but could not complete the test due to a gas tube failure early into test-

the barrel would be measured occasionally but was not considered a vital measurement for purposes of these tests. The temperatures would be measured in the Fahrenheit scale with a Geneva Scientific Model TLL950LS Infrared thermometer. This thermometer has a working temperature range from -32° up to +950° and no contact is necessary to slow down the testing or require cumbersome embedded sensors.

Since we determined that it was going to be possible to reach a catastrophic failure point, for safety purposes, each test rifle was fitted with a KNS precision tripod adapter allowing it to be fired from a standard MG42 anti-aircraft tripod, and both series of tests also employed a set of KNS Precision Spade grips. This combination would allow the shooter to place his body well behind the action of the firearm and not require a cheek weld on the stock only inches from the chamber.

We decided to use Wolf 62-grain, FMJ .223 for several reasons. First, there was an abundance on hand, and if both test rifles reached their maximum number of rounds allotted for the testing, we would need at least 2,000 rounds. Secondly, and most importantly, this was to be one hell of an endurance test and it is almost universally agreed that steel-cased ammunition has the potential to be tougher on chambers than traditional, brass-cased ammo. Contrary to sometimes popular internet and urban legend, we have run tens of thousands of rounds of this ammo during testing firearms of all calibers, types and styles over the years with no adverse effects whatsoever.

A "before" photo with several loaded drums and stripper clips in preparation for testing. The PACT timer & chronograph was used to make sure the firearms tested functioned with a similar rate of fire before testing. The Geneva Scientific infrared thermometer can be seen at the back right.

Load Up

All available BETA C-Mags were loaded and the remainder of the ammo was loaded onto steel stripper clips for use with a speed loader. We didn't know really what to expect, but having heard stories about "fire till failure" drills with other rifles, we dressed properly including correct sight and hearing protection. The 16-inch barreled P-416 was mounted on the MG42 anti-aircraft tripod and the baseline temperatures were taken. The air temperature was a seasonal 41° above zero with no measurable wind and all parts to be checked were very close to our established "room temperature" this day. (A complete set of charts with all round counts and recorded temperatures are included with this article). After establishing that everything was at a base temperature, it was time for the testing to start.

Drum number 1 was loaded and emptied in a single, sub 10-second burst. This was the kind of shooting that we were always warned against because it was potentially destructive and usually pointless in situations where "placing multiple hits on approaching targets was necessary." It is also precisely the kind of shooting that many serious class III recreational shooters (who have no current approaching enemy targets at the time) really enjoy. The rifle was quickly cleared and temperature measurements were taken in the chamber area, the bolt face, the gas block and the muzzle brake. All were recorded and the next drum was loaded in approximately 90 seconds time.

The bolt was closed on drum number 2 and it was emptied as flawlessly as the first. Measurements were repeated, the next drum was loaded. As the P-416 effortlessly continued to chug along through drums 3, 4, 5, 6, 7 and 8, we wondered if it would indeed make the 1,000-round count we set without a major stoppage.

Drum 9 ran as smooth as the first and it wasn't until approximately 1/3 into the 10th and final drum that the rhythmic sounds we were getting quite used to screeched to a halt. A quick survey of the situation showed nothing more than a severely cracked magazine feed tower had allowed it to spread and log jam several rounds up inside the action. The loose rounds were quickly cleared and an 11th full magazine was immediately inserted, giving way to another 100-round stream of steel casings, that never ended until the magazine was empty. The final readings were taken and the Phase II portion of the P-416 test was officially over. We didn't have any reason to believe it would not make it through the whole 1,000 rounds in this harsh manor, but we were still relieved and impressed that it did. A count of the rounds fired through the malfunctioning magazine gave us a total of 1,036 rounds fired throughout the test.

Phase II, Part II

All the data gathered during the P-416 portion was quickly filed, and a second rifle was brought out to duplicate the testing with, and to take direct comparative measurements from, while in exactly the same conditions. This second rifle was a standard direct impingement system with an M4 contoured 16-inch barrel, and utilized the same lower receiver and mount setup for continuity.

After taking baseline temperatures the shooting began in the same manner as the first rifle. The first BETA C-Mag was inserted and the first 100-round magazine dump was completed as easily as with the first rifle. It was getting a little darker at this point and the glowing gas tube was highly visible under the rail system. We quickly swooped in with the instrumentation, gathered the necessary numbers and we were onto the second burst.

Drum number 2 was inserted, the bolt was dropped and the range filled again with the same rhythmic beat that had been played since we were set up and started the testing. The gas tube started glowing almost simultaneously with the beginning of the firing, evidenced by the residual heat in it, the barrel and the gas block. The cyclic rate remained smooth and even, and all 100 rounds found their mark in the impact area. The numbers were gathered and drum number 3 was inserted.

As soon as the impact area was in the sights the trigger was engaged and drum 3 was on its way to being rapidly emptied. The gas tube again glowed immediately, and this time the cyclic rate was almost instantly erratic. About 30 rounds into the third drum the cyclic rate started slowing and eventually sputtered to a stop. Pulling the charging handle rearward, an empty chamber was discovered. There had been a gas tube failure and there was not enough pressure to bring the bolt carrier back far enough to pick up a new round and chamber it. Another round was cycled by hand and fired only to have the same result. The magazine was pulled, the gun cleared, and the measurements recorded. Test over. The total rounds fired in the second rifle was 264.

Heat Transfer

As discovered through the measurements we recorded, heat was indeed transferred into the action of the firearm through the gas tube at a much faster rate than with the piston gun. The numbers that seemed to indicate the most significant difference were the temperatures of the bolt itself. The bolt face temperature was measured after every magazine was emptied and it reached a higher temperature after firing only 200 rounds with the direct impingement gun than it did even after firing over 1,000 rounds through the piston gun. Another factor that plays into the equation is friction, which is greatly reduced in the P-416 by the removal of the gas rings and the silicone nickel coating, which creates an extremely smooth surface.

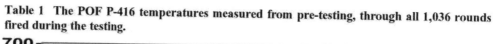

Table 1 The POF P-416 temperatures measured from pre-testing, through all 1,036 rounds fired during the testing.

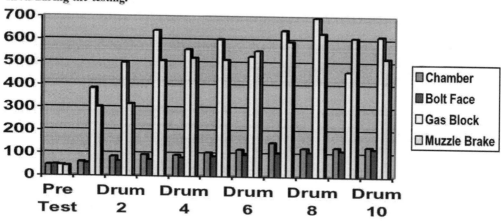

Chamber temperatures recorded with the direct impingement rifle reached a maximum of 115° and was recorded after 264 rounds, the maximum number of rounds fired. The P-416 reached a similar temperature of 119° after firing 600 rounds. All temperatures were measured in the rear of the chamber through the barrel extension.

Table 2 The direct impingement rifle temperatures measured from pre-testing through the end of the testing. Testing was halted at 264 rounds due to gas tube failure.

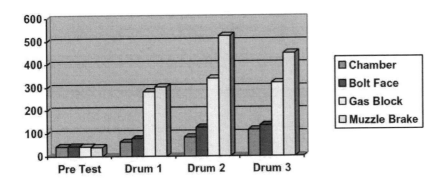

The gas block of the P-416 retained much more heat after firing than the gas block of the direct impingement rifle. While the maximum temperature recorded with the direct impingement rifle was after only 200 rounds, it only reached a temperature of 339°. After firing 200 rounds in the P-416, the gas block reached a temperature of 498° and spiked at 697° after firing 800 rounds. Gas block temperatures fluctuated greatly throughout the testing but seemed to dissipate much faster in the direct impingement rifle. The mass of the gas block is much greater in the P-416 and the free flowing transfer of heat ends there in that particular system as opposed to allowing the flow rearward through means of the gas tube.

Conclusion

We did not really know what to expect when we started this test. The number of rounds fired in the short time allowed was way beyond the normal use of any standard black rifle. The rifle system itself was simply not designed to fire that many rounds without failure. We have all seen enough melted gas tubes and have a good enough understanding of how the system works to know this kind of abuse is well past its intended use. The point of the test was to fire as many rounds as the rifle would withstand, and record the data to that point. Since the P-416 was still functioning at the end of the testing, we still do not know what that end point really is. Maybe a "fire till failure" test is something we should explore in the future. All this writer knows for certain is that the POF-USA P-416 rifle system was designed without the limitations of a standard black rifle and continues to perform in ways quite unrealistic to the original design. There seems to be plenty of active debate about the piston operating system versus the direct impingement design and there may never be a "perfect" system for everyone. Just like there are desired barrel lengths, calibers and mounting platforms that some see as mission critical and others see as simple options, the operating system may just be another choice for the end user to determine and remain the topic of another endless debate in the gun world. While there may be valid reasons to stick with a time proven direct impingement system in some instances, it is clearly becoming obvious to some that the newly designed piston systems on the market today also have definite advantages. It was not very long ago that the implication of a rifle that could double as a PDW and a SAW would be considered unrealistic at best. Today, thanks to POF-USA, that might not seem quite so far-fetched.

High Capacity, Heavy Endurance & Accuracy Retention

The POF-USA P416 Test - Phase III

If you are a regular reader of Small Arms Review, you may remember the first introduction to the POF-USA P416. In the September, 2006 issue (Vol. 9, No. 12) we ran the results of a long term endurance test. We decided to punish a 9.25-inch barreled P416 and recorded over 9,000 rounds of fully automatic fire, many in large bursts, without cleaning. The test was ended when we encountered the first failure to eject. It turned out that it was a faulty magazine that "squirted" several rounds into the action of the gun and the same magazine malfunctioned in the next gun it was inserted in.

The second phase of the testing took place and was published in the March, 2008 issue (Vol. 11, No. 6) of SAR. In this test we brought a 16-inch barreled P416, a traditional direct gas impingement (DGI) M4 and 2,000 rounds of ammo, loaded in BETA C-Mags. The point of the exercise was to fire 1,000 rounds in each gun in 100-round bursts and, using a Geneva Scientific infrared thermometer, make several heat measurements between each reloading. We ended up shooting 1,036 rounds through the P416 due to a magazine malfunction in the middle of one of the strings without failure. The M4 ended up recording 264 rounds due to a catastrophic failure to the gas tube.

Since the last series of tests, both of the P416 examples have endured plenty of heavy use. The 9.25-inch barreled gun has topped the 50,000-round mark and continues to run at every outing to the range. The 16-inch gun has endured far less fire but is still over the 4,000-round mark. Both guns remain very dirty with minimal cleaning, if any, and the idea to check another very important factor happened by chance.

While attending an Armorer's Class for AR-15/M16/M4 rifles a year or so ago, when the class was over we were checking chambers of numerous guns with a chamber gauge. Since the 9.25-inch P416 was in the author's immediate possession, the instructor was asked if it could be brought in and gauged. After explaining the punishment it has endured, most of us expected to see the chamber gauge drop halfway down the barrel. To say we were very surprised when the chamber checked out just fine is an understatement. It was at this point the third test came to mind.

The only thing we have yet to check after punishing these guns is the retained accuracy, if any is left, after these grueling tests. From a "practical accuracy" standpoint, the 9.25-inch gun is the author's "go to" gun (yes, even after all that punishment) and it has been used to run several instructor qualification rounds and used to win several SMG competitions. We know the practical accuracy is still there but most drills are fairly close and fast moving. That's when we decided to see just how well the 16-inch gun could really perform.

The P416 in the 100-yard accuracy phase of testing.

We have all heard about barrels being "shot out" and it certainly happens. The author has witnessed "Constant Lomont" completely destroy a few barrels in his legendary belt runs of the past at the Knob Creek Shots. While the damaged subjects have usually been Browning machine guns that keep on chugging, an inspection of the impact area shows more rounds hitting sideways than strait on. So, due to our own experience we know it is certainly possible, but the term "shot out" seems to be thrown around fairly freely in gun shop conversations and on Internet forums. As an example, after the airing of a current television reality show where a participant ran three consecutive 100-round bursts through a black rifle, many gun forums lit up on the Internet discussing how the gun must be ruined now, even though it was still running at the end because it was "shot out" and several people chimed in about just how much punishment a barrel could handle before the rifling was deemed ineffective.

Range Time

The 16-inch barreled P416 has been a host to a rail mounted LMT M203 40mm grenade launcher. It has been used with iron sights, specifically a removable carry handle with standard E3 rear sight and a POF FTA 2005 front sight. The carry handle is a Stag Arms left-hand version so the attachment knobs do not interfere with the M203 Quadrant Sight. Hardly a "match rifle" configuration but it has always done well putting rounds into any unsuspecting container of Tannerite that happened to be placed in the target area.

Table 1 The POF P-416 temperatures measured from pre-testing, through all 1,036 rounds fired during the testing.

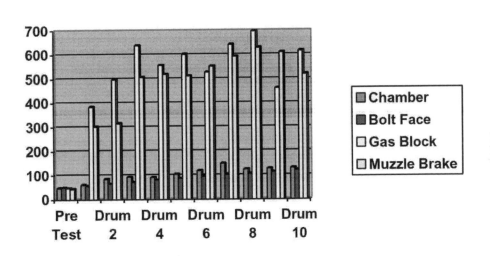

The first thing we needed to do was clean the rifle and barrel. Then we decided not to, since we have recorded such amazing results running dirty, like advertised. Ammo to be used this day was 55-grain Federal XM193. We removed the carry handle and quadrant sight and replaced it with a Bushnell Holo-Sight. After a brief sighting in period it was time for some serious business. We set up at 50 yards, using the M203 as a barrel rest and fired several 3-shot and 5-shot groups. With low expectations when we approached the targets, our uncertainty fast turned to surprise. There were several groups in the 1-inch and under 1-inch size. We changed sights and added a Trijicon ACOG with identical results. So much for a 1,000-round exercise fired in 100-round bursts creating a "shot out" barrel situation.

The second part of our accuracy test was to replace the optics yet again and move to a further firing point. We sighted in a Leupold M8 Tactical scope and moved back to the 100-yard point. Continuing to use the XM193 ammo we ran into an unexpected situation. Due to the gradual downward slope of the range we could no longer use the M203 for a barrel rest. We needed to bring the platform down lower to achieve the point of aim we needed. In the absence of any 20-round magazines we were forced to use 30-round magazines or to load each round individually. We chose the first option and simply used the magazine as a monopod for shooting at 100 yards. Several 5-shot groups were fired, all coming in under the 2-inch mark. Considering that the 55-grain XM193 ammo isn't renown for it's "match accuracy" and combined with our 30-round P-Mag "monopod" shooting style with a dirty gun that has endured such extreme use, it was considered it may end up being "disposable" when we started the first testing but we were quite impressed with these results.

After these initial findings we decided to clean up our act and start taking these tests even more serious. This initial exercise shattered our original expectations and we still remain amazed at the performance we were recording given the previous factors. We know these guns perform very well with Hornady ammo, and we intended to return the following day with a clean barrel, plenty of ammo, a proper magazine for accurate shooting, and a BW Optic Y-Tac scope. Mother Nature, however, had different plans. After a "surprise" April Fool's Day storm dumped over a foot of heavy new snow it was determined this latest test would end at this point. There are several factors we can control but "Mother Nature" and "Father Deadline" take precedent of the print schedule.

We will continue with these tests in the future and see how well this "shot-up" platform can still perform, this time with all the benefits of a true accuracy test.

SAW or Rifle? Maybe both!

Keeping with the theme of the original testing we decided this P416 was a very appropriate platform for testing the new 150-round Armatac SAW-MAG. We "just happened" to have one with us, as well

The 150-round SAW-MAG weighs in at 3.9 pounds. It is constructed of a long glass high impact fiber with a steel USGI tower. It is much lighter and less cumbersome than the original CL-MAG.

as an ample supply of XM193 ammunition for this testing.

The SAW-MAG is the latest evolution of the earlier CL-MAG designed by Armatac Industries. We have been shooting the original CL-MAGs for a few years when we got the call from Armatac to "hold the presses" and wait for the latest and greatest version of their high-capacity feeding device. While waiting for this latest version to arrive we wondered how it could differ from the original. When it showed up it was an obvious upgrade.

In general terms, the SAW-MAG is a single feed, duel drum 150-round magazine for any firearm in the AR-15/M16/M4 family. It is manufactured from a long glass high impact fiber and incorporates a steel USGI tower. A feature that immediately caught our eye was the bold statement "No Lubrication." Since the P416 family also boasts "Lubrication Optional" and has proven beyond doubt in several platforms that it is far more than a catch phrase, we thought it might be a good match with this drum magazine. Beyond that, the sustained fire the P416 system has endured in heavy testing has proven it can easily handle such a large capacity of ammo without the normal failure rate of a DGI black rifle system. Our intuition proved to be accurate.

The first pleasant surprise in using the SAW-MAG happened immediately after arriving at the range. Knowing that all our test gear was

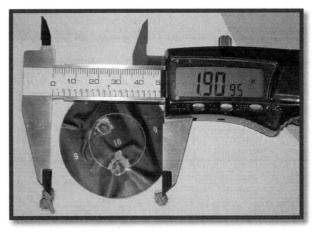

100-yard, 5-shot groups with the Federal XM193 still measured smaller than 2 inches even with the "less than ideal" conditions. At this stage in the testing the rifle had already undergone the Heavy Fire Endurance Test of firing over 1,000 rounds in 100-round bursts in fully automatic, followed by several thousand more rounds with no barrel cleaning.

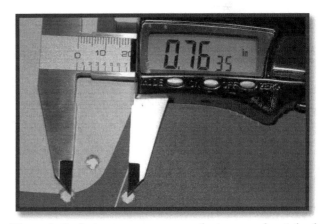

50-yard, 3-shot groups measured at or under 1-inch repeatedly when using sights with little or no magnification following the Heavy Fire Endurance Test.

at the range we did not pack a magazine loader and after a very short inventory it was originally thought that we may have overlooked this important tool. While another member of our test team went looking through the equipment trailer for the loader the author started loading the SAW-MAG by hand. Much to our astonishment it was an easy load, to full capacity with no loader at all. The normal loader was subsequently located though not necessary beyond its timesaving characteristics.

The SAW-MAG is available in a carry bag that is MOLLE compatible to current military gear. The SAW-MAG is designed so that it may be fired while inside the carry bag and does not need to be removed. It also has a carry strap that can be used to support and balance the loaded weapon. All of our testing to date has been used while the magazine is inside the carry bag and we have not found any situation where the carry bag is a hindrance.

The first question we keep hearing when bringing the SAW-MAG out to test is always the same; "When would that much capacity be useful for a standard M16 shooter? Doesn't the SAW gunner handle that role?" Well, let's think about this a little. Since the SAW-MAG fits in a standard AR-15/M16/M4 family rifle, every shooter has the ability to be a "SAW gunner" if the situation should arise that they need the additional firepower without any modifications necessary. It doesn't hang any lower than a traditional 30-round magazine so shooting positions and styles do not need to be greatly altered from original training.

The second question that follows is more of a statement, being; "That must weigh a ton!" The answer here is also surprising. The magazine weighs in at 3.9 pounds. When loaded and attached to a 416, the total weight is 17 pounds. As a reference, an unloaded M249 SAW weighs 17 pounds. For the role it can offer to fill, the weight doesn't seem as much of a factor with a little research.

Shooting the SAW-MAG

As mentioned earlier, the loading is a simple procedure, replicating that of a regular GI magazine. A loading tool makes it faster but is not necessary. Its size was not the downfall we anticipated by any means. When trying to shoot it exactly like a carbine with a 20-round GI magazine it was much heavier and difficult to steady. In situations where the user would be utilizing a SAW-MAG, a prone style, much like that of a 249 SAW is much more practical. It can be used with a normal bipod but since we had an M203 grenade launcher on our test rifle we chose to rest the rifle on the SAW-MAG and it was comfortable and very stable with no malfunctions in any mode of fire. The SAW-MAG was designed for prone use and gets high marks in this area.

Many may note that extremely heavy fire, especially with a high capacity magazine and in long bursts, can be detrimental to a standard DGI platform gun. The gas-tube failures we recorded earlier have been over 250 rounds, and seldom as low as 150 rounds, even in a single burst, which is unusual in a military situation, and almost never without an additional contributing factor such as severe gas port erosion. When used in the POF-USA P415 and P416 weapon system the high capacity, even in heavy fire situations, should never prove to be an issue. If your gun runs fast you shouldn't have to worry about the drum keeping up, as it is tested to 2,000 rounds per minute (rpm).

Since the introduction of the original CL-MAG, the earliest version of the SAW-MAG, several upgrades have been implemented. This latest version is more durable, less cumbersome, compatible with standard military MOLLE gear, requires no lubrication, is very uncomplicated to use and maintain, and is much less expensive. That is a big list of upgrades in a very short amount of time.

There are a few more upgrades and options that will be available very soon in the SAW-MAG family. A round counter is almost ready for release and a smaller version, the 78-round SAW-LITE is close to the marketplace. Small Arms Review will keep you updated on these developments as they are brought to our attention. The MSRP of the new Armatac Industries 150-round SAW-MAG is far less than the earlier, original designs at only $389.99.

Conclusions

The POF-USA P416 family of firearms has continued to impress our test team in the very abusive treatment it has withstood and it continues to impress as more testing continues. To have a firearm that will withstand the punishment we continuously inflict is remarkable. To have the same firearm retain the ability to slip back to its role as a dependable and an accurate rifle after being used and abused far past it's recommended or traditional standards of use is astonishing. It seems that the P416 pushes the envelope at every attempt and continues to function as though it has been heavily maintained and infrequently fired, instead of the exact opposite.

When a product like the 150-round SAW-MAG can be combined with the P416 weapon system and it can serve in multiple roles, and excel in all roles, we should take notice. The P416 / SAW-MAG combination can handily fill the role of a SAW and a standard issue M4, without being manufactured to function in a limited use when crossing into the role of another system; at much less weight for one role with much more performance in both situations. The accuracy retention during and after heavy use is noteworthy, and the fact that the P416 is a familiar platform with very few mechanical differences and almost no function changes to the same weapon system our soldiers and operators have been trained on as our primary service weapon for almost 5 decades. This brings a superior performance without any major training changes for the operator, and only a few minor changes from the armorer's perspective, all rolled into a single weapon system. The addition of the SAW-MAG in our early testing, to this already proven workhorse only propels these results higher.

Since it has been our experience over several years of testing that this level of performance is not an anomaly or an abnormality, maybe we have reached the point where it is time for the standards to be brought up to the abilities of these new weapon systems rather than be impressed at the superior performance as they completely surpass the levels of performance considered standard for so long.

Spade Grips for the Black Rifle from KNS Precision

From .22LR to .50 BMG, with barrel lengths from just a few inches to over three feet, the AR-15/M16 continues to evolve with every passing day. No stranger to this particular weapon system, KNS Precision, Inc. has taken it to yet another level by designing and marketing a spade grip mechanism that will work on all AR-15 style rifles with no permanent modifications to the firearm. The reasonable price and availability of high capacity feeding devices including newer belt-fed units have made the concept even more desirable.

The instructions are simple and easy to follow and the unit can be quickly installed with minimal difficulty by the end user. All factory internal parts are utilized with the KNS Spade Grip assembly and the lower receiver never has to be disassembled. The only time anything resembling disassembly is necessary is if the host firearm has a full stock. The KNS D-Grip is designed to be used with a carbine length buffer tube and buffer, which are included with the kit, and must be utilized to fit and function properly.

After the kit was installed and adjusted, it was time for range trials. Not being satisfied with shooting this configuration on a bipod, a mount was designed to allow the use of an M60 "Gooseneck" pintle in any standard 30-caliber pintle receiver. A special vehicle mount was earlier developed to fit into a 2-inch Reese Hitch receiver for vehicle applications, which was also used in this testing. For this particular project a pintle receiver for use with an MG42 anti-aircraft tripod was fabricated. (Since this time KNS also developed, and now offers, their own MG42 AA tripod mount for use with any railed forend).

Range Time

Arrows at indicate the exterior trigger area that must be depressed to fire the weapon. Arrow at (B) is the internal trigger linkage that is pulled to the rear engaging the rifle trigger when external trigger (A) is depressed.

Time spent on the range with the KNS M16 D garnered a lot of attention. It looks drastically different than most "traditional" firearms and doesn't really fit the mold for the AR-15/M16 family of firearms. Everyone who had the opportunity to fire it immediately enjoyed it, especially since it was used in conjunction with a registered, fully automatic lower receiver and a variety of upper receivers. Combined with a Beta C-Mag, smiles were abundant. Although we used a fully automatic firearm for a host for the purposes of this article, it was designed to work fine with a semiautomatic version as well.

It was found that trigger control and discipline would be necessary with the first of several melted gas-tubes. That was quickly rectified in a number of ways. It is important to remember that this modification only pertains to the lower receiver so when things started to get too hot, we switched to an MGI QCB Upper Receiver and swapped out the barrels with fresh ones before they got to the failure point. All that was necessary was to throw two levers, pull out the barrel, slide in the new barrel and close the levers. At that point it was functioning a little more like a Squad Automatic Weapon than a standard M16.

A few other upper receivers were also utilized during testing and the system just seemed to get more interesting and unique as the shooting commenced. When fitted with a 16-inch POF Gas Piston Upper, all the heat and gas tube troubles went away. The 16-inch version was chosen over the 9.25-inch unit due to the attractive slower cyclic rate. One Beta C-Mag could be fired after another without any adverse effect on the firearm in this configuration.

Another assembly that worked well was the Lakeside Guns LM-7 upper receiver. This is the .22LR upper that feeds from cloth belts or nylon links. To shoot this as a belt-fed, with spade grips, feed box and link catcher seemed very natural and ranked extremely high on the fun scale.

Conclusion

After using the KNS Spade Grip, this writer believes it has a permanent home in his reference collection. It is well made, easy to install and easily removable if the operator desires the temporary replacement of the collapsible stock should they desire to return to the original configuration. It functions well and worked with everything we combined it with for additional accessories. It was evaluated clearly from a recreational standpoint and all who utilized it, giving it high marks, were simply sandpit commandos (recreational shooters) like the author. It was not evaluated for tactical or professional applications nor was it relayed by the manufacturer that it was developed with those uses in mind. For the "shooter who has everything" and likes to be the first on his range with something fun and new, the KNS Precision Spade Grips come highly recommended. MSRP $449.99

The Bloom Automatic Golf Ball Launcher

Thanks to Vince Bloom, Your Golf Game Never Looked Better!

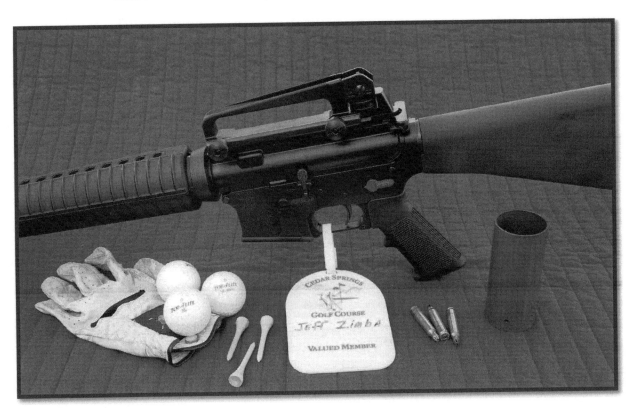

Imagine standing on the Tee area of your favorite Par 4 hole and wishing you could get to the green in 1. (Putting for Eagle is something that most of us never have the chance do). You reach into your bag and select your 20-inch Colt H-Bar. As you drop your Top-Flite XL-3000 ball into the Bloom muzzle device, you read the wind and aim a little to the left to compensate for it. With a hollow sounding thump your ball takes flight and bounces just short of the green, rolling up beside the pin. It looks like another day of shooting under par.

We don't know how your local golf course will feel about using the Bloom Automatic Golf Ball Launcher but we have yet to encounter a shooting range that doesn't allow it.

The Bloom Automatic Golf Ball Launcher is a muzzle attachment designed to be used with several firearms. Rather than having a dedicated thread that must be matched to a particular firearm, this device will function with any standard 22mm flash hider or grenade launcher. It simply slides over the factory flash hider or grenade launcher and is secured with dog-point set screws in the corresponding grooves. Unlike cup-point set screws, there should be no scratching or marring of the original finish.

The firearms the Bloom device can be used with include, but are not limited to, the following unmodified firearms; Yugo SKS, AR-15, M16, FAL, Galil, CETME, G-3 and MAS 49/56. It will also function on the 1903 Springfield, M1 Garand and M1A / M14 when used in conjunction with their grenade launching attachments. They also recently added the correct flash hiders for an AK47 to use with this system.

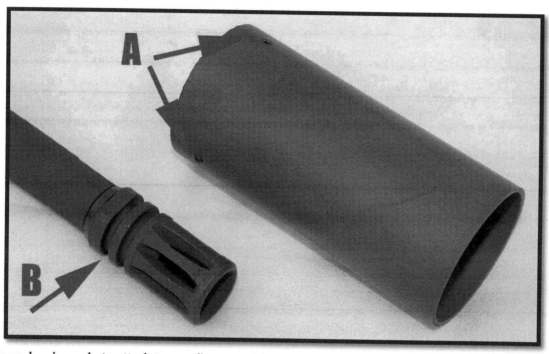

The launcher is made to attach to any firearm with a 22mm flash hider. It uses dog-point set screws (A) and is simply secured on one of the rings (B) on the flash hider.

After securing the launcher to the firearm, all that is necessary is a bucket of golf balls and a corresponding number of blanks. For obvious reasons this device should NEVER be used with live ammunition. A golf ball is dropped into the launcher and the blank round is loaded into the chamber. To fire, hold the rifle on your shoulder in a slightly elevated position so the ball will not roll out.

The distance the ball will travel depends entirely upon the caliber and the barrel length of the firearm used. With a 20-inch barrel on an AR-15 the balls can fly as far as 350 yards. When used with an 11.5-inch barrel, the distance was reduced to somewhere in the area of 100 - 150 yards. With an SKS they will fly in excess of 500 yards; almost completely out of sight. We can only assume that when used with the M1A or M1 Garand they will travel further. Standard blanks are used in conjunction with the Bloom Automatic Golf Ball Launcher and the use of grenade launching blanks is not recommended.

Something that has to be considered when firing golf balls is that they react unpredictably when they strike a hard surface. It would not be recommended to fire at a hard surface where there is the potential for the ball to bounce back towards the shooter or any spectators.

During our testing we found it fun to place several 5-gallon pails in a large area and try to see if we could drop any balls in the pails. Other suggested "sporting" options would be to use 55-gallon drums or paint large circles in the field or range in a bulls-eye fashion and, in a 21st Century version of "Jarts," hits could be scored by their proximity to the target. While there is no tactical factor being sold with this attachment, the fun factor is certainly high, and with a little imagination several competitive and recreational uses can be discovered.

In support of this neat accessory, Bloom Automatic is going to offer blank crimp dies for sale. This will assist the reloaders who wish to manufacture their own loads instead of purchasing factory blanks, which at times can be elusive and expensive. Some factory blanks can be corrosive and reloading will solve that concern.

There has been a lot of discussion about specific launching accessories and their rulings within the Technology Branch of the ATF. As of this writing, ATF has ruled that the Bloom Automatic Golf Ball Launcher does not constitute a firearm or a destructive device. This conclusion followed a 6-month discussion period with the ATF legal department and they have even issued a ruling letter to this effect. A copy of this ruling is available at the Bloom Automatic website:

There are several new platforms for the launcher to be used on and they now include the 1911 pistol and some of the MAC family of firearms. All of this new information is available on their website as well. The price for the standard launcher, as tested in Small Arms Review magazine is $40 with an additional $5 shipping fee.

The Hydra Modular Weapon System from MGI

Very few firearms can claim to be as versatile as the AR-15/M16. Thanks to MGI the spectrum just widened even more - much more.

There is an abundance of caliber conversions, barrel lengths and configuration options available for the firearm that has been the primary service weapon of the United States military for over 40 years. In order to make such radical changes to a single rifle, it has been necessary to procure a new, barreled upper receiver, a matching rail system, and specialty magazines with proprietary adapters. At least that used to be the case - until now. Enter the Hydra Modular Weapons System from MGI Military, Inc.

Imagine having one firearm, in this case a registered M16, and having the ability to fire numerous calibers. That is not such a big stretch since several conversions in the form of barreled upper receivers have been available for a number of years. What if you could make the caliber change in less than 2 minutes without using any tools? Again, nothing very spectacular because changing the barreled upper receiver and bolt is a fast and easy process. What if you could do this and continue using your upper receiver and rail system without even having to disassemble the firearm? Now that is something radically different.

In the Beginning

The Hydra Modular Weapons System is a combination of AR-15/M16/M4 upgrades going back for decades. Mack Gwinn Jr., President of MGI Military, Inc. holds over 25 firearms related patents. The original founder of several firearms related companies including Bushmaster Firearms and MWG, Gwinn has been involved in the firearms industry for almost 4 decades. While many of his designs are unrelated to the AR-15/M16/M4, such as the M2HB-QCB, his latest venture, MGI certainly focuses on this weapons system and boasts impressive upgrades and radical design changes.

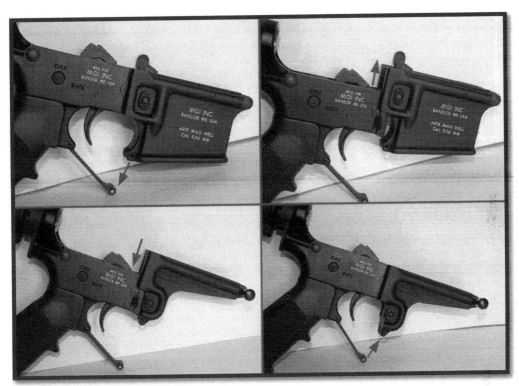

In order to change the magazine well, all the operator needs to do is (A) depress the trigger guard detent and swing the guard down. (B) Depress the magazine release button and lift the magazine well up and off the receiver. (C) Place the new magazine well down on the receiver, aligning the dovetail slots until it snaps and locks onto the magazine release. (D) Replace the trigger guard.

The Upper Receiver

As reviewed in Small Arms Review (Vol. 8, No. 3, December 2004) the MGI Quick Change Barrel (QCB) Upper Receiver allows the shooter the ability to quickly change barrels with no tools in less than a minute. The QCB Upper Receiver has undergone several upgrades and modifications in the last two and a half years, including a complete rail system as the standard handguard. The MGI QCB-C handguard utilizes four 5.75-inch M1913 Picatinny rails, each at 3 o'clock, 6 o'clock, 9 o'clock and 12 o'clock. The 12 o'clock (top) rail is completely regulated with the flattop rail on the upper receiver giving the operator several sight and accessory options. They are manufactured so precise that the upper and handguard can even be "bridged" creating a top rail over 13 inches in length when used with a carbine length barrel and gas system. For those who wish to use a full-length barrel and gas system, MGI also offers a 5.5-inch handguard/rail extension. When utilizing this extension the top rail is almost 19 inches in length.

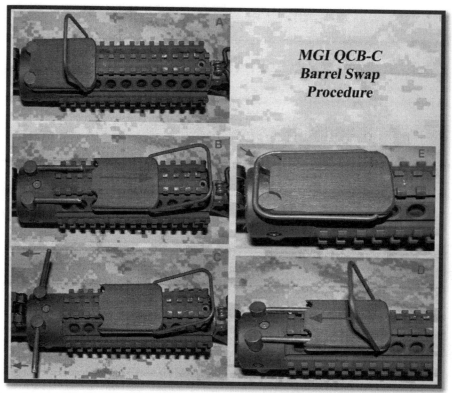

With a barrel in place, lock or hold the bolt to its rearward position and snap the retaining lock (A) up. Slide the retaining block (B) to the front to expose the locking arms. Swing the arms (C) open and the barrel will slide out to the front. To install the new barrel, reverse the procedure. Snapping the retaining lock back down € completes the barrel change procedure.

Another major upgrade to the new MGI QCB-C Upper Receiver is the addition of the barrel locking arm retaining block. This retaining block slides on the 6 o'clock Picatinny rail and slides over the barrel locking arms, holding them firmly and eliminating anything sticking out that could be caught on clothing or foliage.

Like the original QCB Upper Receiver the new QCB-C variation still uses factory AR-15/M16/M4 barrels. There is nothing proprietary that needs to be purchased to use this system. If you have a factory barrel you wish to use with the QCB Upper Receiver, all you need to do is remove the delta ring, the barrel nut, the sling swivel and the front handguard keeper and it is ready to use. No special parts or accessories are necessary and all existing barrels work fine. In the case of changing calibers as well

110

as barrel lengths the correct bolt and bolt carrier are installed and the upper receiver conversion is complete.

The Lower Receiver

Most people would agree that the weakest link in AR-15/M16/M4 caliber conversions is the feeding system. The shape, function and interior dimensions of the original magazine-well don't easily allow the use of many other magazines. When others are utilized, special and sometimes expensive adapters are typically necessary, and at times, mandate the use of heavily customized proprietary magazines. These can also be quite expensive since they are not surplus or even "off the shelf" items. The performance with some of them has also been less than acceptable at times due to the constraints of the original magazine-well dimensions. When there are problems, magazine related feeding and function issues always seem to lead to the majority of the troubles. Anyone who has tried to push several 7.62x39mm rounds into a standard 30-round AR-15 magazine and expect it to feed reliably when used with a 7.62x39 upper receiver has undoubtedly faced the same problems. In this particular situation, the larger diameter of the rounds necessitates more curvature in the feeding device in order to freely advance and feed correctly. The straight shape of a factory AR-15/M16/M4 magazine-well does not allow for this magazine shape.

This major feeding problem has been resolved with the MGI Hydra Modular Weapon System by simply allowing the user to utilize the correct magazine for the correct caliber. This gives the proper presentation of the cartridge in both height and feed angle, as it was originally designed for, using factory magazines. When shooting 5.56x45 (.223 Rem), standard AR-15 magazines are used. When converting to 7.62x39mm, standard AK47 magazines are used. When shooting .45ACP, Grease Gun magazines are used and when using a 9x19mm system, Sten magazines (and soon Glock, Uzi and Colt magazines) can be utilized. All these magazines work in their original, unmodified condition, and all without the use of expensive and troublesome magazine-well adapters.

This advancement in the MGI Hydra feed system has been accomplished by designing the lower receiver to accept several magazine-wells, so the correct magazine can always be used with the correct caliber, bolt and barrel. The magazine-well can be removed and replaced with no tools and easily accomplished in under 1 minute. At the present time, magazine-wells are available in 5.56x45mm (.223 Rem) and 7.62x39 with others in the final stages of production including 9x19mm and 45ACP. Provisions for several other calibers are also being developed including .22LR, .22 Magnum, .40 S&W, 7.62x25mm and many more.

The Complete Modular System

Even though the MGI QCB Upper Receiver is completely compatible with all Mil-Spec AR-15/M16/M4 lower receivers, and the MGI Modular Lower Receiver is compatible with all Mil Spec upper receivers, the real potential of their flexibility happens when they are used in conjunction with each other. Several other components have also been developed and designed to be used in this system and when combined, create entirely new possibilities and options that never existed in the past.

The Defender D-Ring

The addition of the MGI "Defender" D-Ring is standard in all complete weapons systems. The D-Ring increases the reliability of the AR-15/M16/M4 by virtually eliminating extraction problems and increases typical extractor spring force by 4 times over the factory spring. The D-Ring is used by several police departments across the nation and is used extensively by members of the armed forces in the War On Terror. Many factors including gas port erosion can contribute to creating a higher rate of fire causing an extreme centrifugal force on the extractor as the bolt rotates and unlocks. This centrifugal force can cause the extractor to lift and can lead to a dangerous failure to extract. The additional force on the extractor keeps it closed in the position it was designed to be in, insuring a positive extraction. Sandy or dirty conditions can also lead to more drag on the casing after firing and this extra spring tension creates a more positive extraction in these cases as well. Over the years, some end users have used common O-rings from the local hardware store to reach the same goal as the D-Ring. While they are inexpensive and plentiful they can lead to a malfunction due to inferior materials compared to the D-Ring. Standard o-rings are not designed to take the harsh and rapid repetitive compression that the D-Ring was engineered for. Also, while the shape of the D-Ring holds it in position, a standard o-ring can slip and cause the extractor to stick open.

The MGI Regulated Gas Tube

The MGI Regulated Gas Tube is another important system upgrade and greatly assists in solving gas port erosion problems. It is completely adjustable allowing the shooter to control the amount of gas used to operate the system. The rifle can be tweaked for particular ammunition or specifically adjusted just for the current conditions it is operating in. It is installed just like a standard gas tube and is adjusted with a standard Allen wrench.

MGI Rate Reducing Buffer

The MGI Rate and Recoil Reducing Buffer assists in increasing hit probability by reducing felt recoil and reducing muzzle rise. These buffers were tested extensively in Small Arms Review (Vol. 7, No. 8, May 2004) and performed extremely well. The buffer utilizes a mechanical operating system and is not sensitive to extreme temperatures like similar hydraulic systems. During all phases of testing, the MGI Rate Reducing Buffer dramatically reduced muzzle rise and consistently lowered the rate of fire when used with fully automatic firearms. The reduction in rate of fire is directly related to the original cyclic rate: the faster the cyclic rate, the greater the reduction in rate of fire. Never did the rate of fire become slow enough where they did not still fire with 100% reliability.

The 7.62x39mm upgrade

While 7.62x39mm conversions to the AR-15/M16/M4 are nothing new, MGI has engineered several improvements to their system. As mentioned previously, the Modular Lower Receiver will accept a magazine-well that allows the use of standard AK47 magazines. In order to function properly with standard AK47 magazines, the bolt carrier has also been slightly modified from the original design. Once modified, the carrier will still work fine when used in conjunction with the 5.56x45mm system so it is actually a multi-use carrier. The MGI QCB-C upper receiver has also been designed to accept these AK47 magazines as well as a multitude of others and has slightly different internal dimensions than standard upper receivers in order to facilitate this conversion.

One of the newest MGI innovations in this caliber conversion is in the fire control group. It is well known that the properties of rifle primers are very different depending on the country of origin and type of ammunition. Some Com-Bloc 7.62x39mm primers can react quite differently than NATO 5.56x45 primers and this difference has led to an unreliability factor when utilized in some firearms. The Com-Bloc firearms designed specifically for this caliber have addressed this in their design and do not have the same reliability issues. After years of research and development MGI believes they have now addressed these differences and will soon be offering a bolt and firing pin upgrade specifically designed for use with this caliber. The author has had the opportunity to test the bolt upgrade in its prototype form, and the results thus far have been excellent. Early tests have shown that when this upgrade is utilized with otherwise unusable ammunition, the failure to fire rate is almost completely diminished. Although this upgrade is designed to be used in conjunction with the MGI Modular Weapons System, it will work with any 7.62x39mm AR-15/M16/M4 conversion to increase reliability.

Range Time

Numerous hours were spent at the range with all aspects of the MGI Hydra Modular Weapons System. While several thousands of rounds have been fired in all configurations, there are a few interesting points that need to be discussed.

One pressing question in particular (and rightly so) always follows a system designed with a quick-change barrel mechanism: "How well does it re-zero after removing and replacing the barrel?" A legitimate question and a series of tests were performed to find that answer when pre-production testing first started.

The tests we designed were far more intense than simply shooting a group, remove barrel, reinstall barrel and re-shoot group exercise. We were looking for and measuring point of impact shift, not sniper grade accuracy. Both barrels were already "well-seasoned" from lots of rate of fire testing and we were running Wolf Polyformance ammunition this day. This was to be conducted as a real-world exercise, not a bench-rest rifle, solenoid-fired electronic trigger test. Rounds would be fired in a rapid-fire fashion, allowing a second or two between each shot but without the luxury of any slow-fire deep breathing exercises like we are all taught to do in NRA Shooting School.

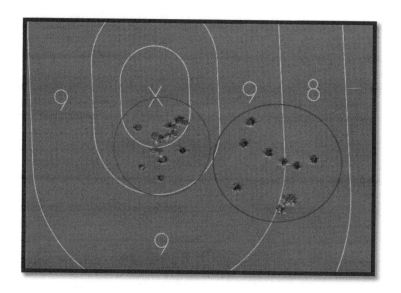

In the left circles are two different 10-round groups of 5.56x45mm ammo, fired individually after completely swapping calibers and firing two 5-round groups of 7.62x39mm ammo as shown in the blue circles. The target above was placed at 50 yard and both groups were fired using the same point of aim. The target below was conducted simultaneously at 100 yards.

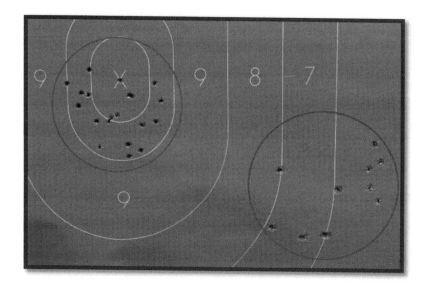

Targets were set at 50 yards and at 100 yards. The rifle was setup in 5.56x45 with a 4x12x40mm scope and was bore-sighted. It was "zeroed" in 5.56x45mm on the 50-yard target. That would be the last of the scope adjustments for this exercise. At 50 yards, ten rounds of 5.56x45mm were fired using the "X" as the point of aim. After letting the barrel cool for just a few seconds the barrel, bolt and magazine-well were swapped out for the 7.62x39mm system. At that point 5 rounds of 7.62x39mm were fired at the 50-yard target using the same point of aim as before. Immediately after firing the 7.62x39mm rounds the rifle was swapped back to 5.56x45mm and another 10 rounds of 5.56x45 were fired again, with the original point of aim. Finishing the 5.56x45, the rifle was converted back to 7.62x39 where we immediately fired 5 more rounds.

We completed the exercise and repeated it exactly the same at 100 yards. We were very pleased with the outcome and surprised at how close the groups were, even though they were completely different barrels and very different calibers. We didn't know what to expect in accuracy as far as the original barrel and ammo combos would be concerned, and were extremely impressed when the original point of impact was re-established after multiple changes. Some photos are included in this article showing the results of these tests. It must be stressed again that these were not accuracy tests, just redundant point of impact tests and the system scored very well. If we used match grade (or even "not-shot-out") barrels with proper trigger time and discipline combined with match ammo we have no doubt the results would be even more dramatic. But that was not the point of this exercise.

The Future

Even though the MGI Hydra Modular Weapon System holds some extremely impressive design characteristics, the project is still in its very early stages and is evolving faster than this writer can keep up. Some of the designs on the drawing board must remain behind closed doors at this time but other upgrades that have been cleared to mention include a belt-feed mechanism, an open bolt option for registered full-auto users and even an open-bolt/closed-bolt system, something many thought could never be developed. The new open-bolt/closed-bolt system is in the final phases of testing and will be entering the pre-production phase very soon. This unique design allows the open-bolt function when utilized in fully automatic and fires in a closed-bolt mode when switched to semiautomatic. This design allows for maximum cooling and increased safety when shooting in fully automatic without compromising accuracy when shooting in semiautomatic. This writer has had the opportunity to handle this upgrade in its various stages and it is very exciting indeed.

Several more calibers and magazine-well options are slowly making their way towards the market. Some additions are as radical as 7.62x51NATO and .458 SOCOM (all based on the same lower receiver and upper receiver design) and some are simply additions to fit more common magazines allowing "duty" magazines to be utilized helping to launch the MGI Hydra Modular Weapon System even higher as a convenient companion rifle for almost any standard "duty" sidearm. To provide an even more unique addition to the system, all pistol calibers are now being tested utilizing the standard gas system instead of the traditional blowback style function that has become so common. In MGI prototype firearms, the early results show far less recoil and better controllability.

Conclusions

The MGI Hydra Modular Weapon System is the most radical and versatile upgrade to the AR-15/M16/M4 that this writer has had the opportunity to handle to date. With numerous caliber changes available and several barrel lengths, all while using standard unmodified barrels with absolutely no tools necessary for changing, it is in a class of its own. Combined with the lower receiver that uses interchangeable magazine-wells allowing common, correct, unmodified magazines with these caliber conversions, this system is well ahead of its time in the standard Black Rifle Market. We are looking forward to additional releases from MGI and will be sure to keep the readers of Small Arms Review informed as they come to the market.

Editor's Note: Due to his involvement in the firearms community, as well as with Small Arms Review magazine, the author is involved with several related businesses in the area of consulting, research & development and testing & evaluation. MGI Military is no exception to this, and due to these unique relationships he is able to provide our readers with first look and premiere article content on occasion.

9mm Suppressed AR-15/M16/M4 Upper Receiver from Coastal Guns

The rifle remains relatively compact at under 30" in overall length as pictured, and still retains the benefit of a sound suppressor with a large volume to aid in sound suppression.

With a POF-USA P-9X Rail System as an exoskeleton and a M.I.M.S. suppressor at the core of the design, the Coastal Guns 9mm upper receiver is not only functional, it is an absolute overachiever.

The explosion in popularity the black rifle has achieved in the last decade has propelled its appeal far outside the circle of military firearm fans who have embraced it for almost 50 years. No longer a simple and modest 5.56mm rifle with the only options being a different stock and barrel length, some configurations are so far removed from the original design they are barely recognizable as AR-15/M16 family firearms. With this broadened appeal come new innovations as the role of the weapon system continues to evolve, and new accessories and caliber conversions are introduced at lightning speed.

While the use of pistol calibers is certainly not a new concept for this firearm, the latest innovation from Coastal Guns bring it to a level not previously achieved. Manufactured as a complete, suppressed 9x19mm upper receiver, it is a true drop-on unit for anyone with a Colt-style 9mm mag-well adapter and heavy buffer. The short 4.75-inch barrel combined with the M.I.M.S. suppressor brings the overall length far under that of a standard 9mm package and at far less cost than the short D.O.E. style upper receiver.

The barrel is free-floating and is completely shrouded by a POF P-9X Predator Rail system. The top rail extends over 16 inches, from the rear of the upper receiver giving the shooter numerous options for sights and optics, and the three additional rails located at 3, 6 & 9 o'clock allow for several accessory options. The side rails measure 8.5 inches in length and the bottom rail is 7.5 inches.

At the heart of the system is the M.I.M.S. silencer and this is where it really starts to break away from many other suppressed pistol caliber systems. Supplied with the correct thread adapter for this upper receiver, the suppressor is completely removable and can be utilized with several other firearm types. The suppressor is not dedicated or "married" to the upper receiver and with the addition of a new Coastal Guns thread adapter it can be used an almost unlimited number of other guns the owner may have. With the potential for a single suppressor to be used on so many firearms the value is enormous considering the number of transfer fees saved, not to mention the price of several silencers otherwise necessary. (See SAR Vol. 12, No. 8, May 2009 for a complete review of the M.I.M.S. silencer system).

Maximum Modularity

As an exercise in modularity we combined the Coastal Guns 9mm upper receiver, complete with a M.I.M.S. suppressor with an MGI Marck-15 Modular Lower Receiver using their "9mm SMG" mag-well. This MGI lower receiver allows the use of multiple magazine wells so it can be calibrated to the desired caliber and magazine without the use of any adapters or special feeding devices. (See SAR Vol.10, No.8, May 2007 for more information on the MGI Modular Lower Receiver.) The 9mm SMG mag-well uses factory Colt 9mm magazines and lightly modified Uzi magazines. To stretch the level of modularity even more we decided to use a .45 ACP M.I.M.S. suppressor with this system. With the identical overall length and diameter of the 9mm M.I.M.S. suppressor, the fit was perfect and the number of firearms it would adapt to would increase several-fold. Our hypothesis was the increased diameter of the baffle internal diameter would be washed out by the large volume of the suppressor. If it proved effective, the value of the system would skyrocket as the number of firearms compatible with the suppressor multiplied.

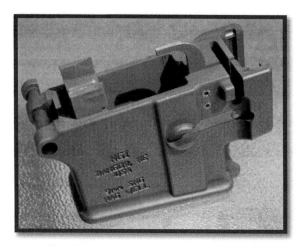

The MGI mag well utilized in the testing with the Coastal Guns 9mm upper receiver. This combination allows the use of factory Colt 9mm magazines with no adapters or modifications.

Range Time

Range time consisted of several days with almost 1,000 rounds fired by numerous shooters. After a very short break-in period of about 60 rounds, the system started to feed and function perfectly. During the first few magazines while running different types of ammunition we experienced some feeding troubles with hollow-point ammo. After a few magazines everything was running well and not another single function problem of any type was experienced during the remainder of the testing. A short break-in period to get things running smooth is not uncommon with a new firearm or component in the experience of the author.

The first thing we checked was also the most obvious. We were all curious whether the M.I.M.S. .45 ACP suppressor would be adequate for the faster and smaller 9mm round or if we were looking for a little too much in the area of modularity and ignoring too much in the performance area. In the absence of any sound metering equipment we had to rely on the second most important measuring tool: our ears. To have something as a baseline to compare against we first used a M.I.M.S. 9mm suppressor and fired a few different types of ammo. After clearing the firearm and removing the 9mm suppressor we installed the .45 ACP M.I.M.S. suppressor and fired the first few rounds. To our delight it was almost indistinguishable from the 9mm can. We started with the heavier and slower 147-grain ammo and worked our way down to the lighter and much faster 115-grain and even 90-grain ammo. It was also extremely similar in sound levels, and was so comfortable that little or no hearing protection was used throughout the remainder of the testing, even when shooting in an enclosed area. The .45 ACP suppressor would reside on the Coastal Guns upper receiver throughout the remainder of the shooting. Since the testing time overlapped a few local shoots, the system was fired by several people who were all quite impressed in all aspects and all had the same response when they looked at the suppressor engraving. The most frequent question uttered by the shooters was: "This is a .45 can?" Our suppression test was deemed a great success.

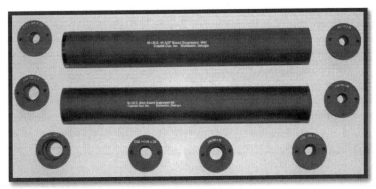

The M.I.M.S. suppressors can be combined with numerous thread adapters allowing their use with a large number of firearms. Pictured are the .45 (top) and 9mm suppressor with the thread adapters available at the time of testing.

The system worked great thus far but just "sounding quiet" and running well wasn't enough to tell us if it was going to be a useful platform. In practical terms, along with going BANG every time you squeeze the trigger, comes hitting what you need to hit, as well. Since the system is a pistol caliber we set up at approximately 50 yards and tested it with five types of ammunition. We measured some five-shot groups and recorded the muzzle velocity of all. The 9x19mm ammunition tested was: SBR GreenMatch 90-grain Frangible, Wolf 115gr FMJ, Winchester 115-grain FMJ, Atlanta Arms 147-grain Subsonic JHP Match and Winchester 147-grain Subsonic JHP.

Five-round groups were fired from a bench and were recorded as follows: Winchester JHP - 1.935 inches; Atlanta Arms JHP - 2.464 inches; SBR GreenMatch Frangible - 3.250 inches; Wolf FMJ - 3.627 inches and Winchester FMJ - 3.759 inches. Given better weather conditions and more time it would be easy to decrease the size of these groups in the opinion of the author. Acknowledging the tiny 4.75 inch barrel of this system, the accuracy at 50 yards was actually quite impressive when compared to other pistol caliber platforms with similar barrel lengths.

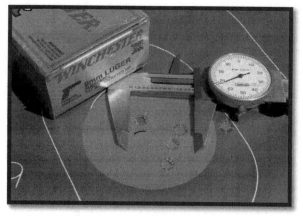

Muzzle velocity was measured from a distance of 8 feet from the end of the suppressor with a PACT MKIV XP Championship Timer & Chronograph. The average MV was recorded as follows: Atlanta Arms JHP - 905 fps; Winchester JHP - 999 fps; Wolf FMJ - 1,120 fps; Winchester FMJ - 1,202 fps and SBR GreenMatch Frangible - 1,226fps.

For a barrel of less than 5" in length, the accuracy was quite impressive when fired from the 50 yard line.

The Legal Stuff

The Coastal Guns 9mm upper receiver utilizes a barrel length of only 4.75 inches in length. The addition of the M.I.M.S. suppressor gives it a perceived barrel length of about 15 inches and it doesn't look grossly short so we thought it was important to mention the following: The Coastal Guns 9mm Upper Receiver can only be used on Title II firearms such as a registered Short Barreled Rifle or registered machine gun. Due to concerns with constructive possession, it is unwise take possession of a short-barreled upper receiver without having either firearm mentioned above. In these days where transferable machine guns are so expensive, registered short-barreled rifles are gaining in popularity and can still be purchased or manufactured for a reasonable amount of money. (For information on registering your own Short Barreled Rifle see SAR Vol. 12, No. 12, September 2009, page 55.)

Summary

The results of this entire experiment in assembling a solid, reliable, modular rifle exceeded our expectations in all areas. The 9mm barreled upper receiver built and assembled by Coastal Guns and matched with their own M.I.M.S. sound suppressor was well thought out and executed. The addition of the POF-USA P-9X rail system to complete the upper receiver solidified it in areas of practicality, performance and even aesthetics. The fit, finish and function of the entire upper receiver system we tested is simply superb.

The Coastal upper receiver with the addition of a small 3x9 mil dot scope used in testing. Although the suppressor gives the illusion of a "normal" barrel length, the barrel is only 4.75" and this upper must only be used on a registered SBR or machine gun.

The use of the .45 ACP M.I.M.S. suppressor with the system absolutely enhances the ability of the owner to multiply the number of suppressed firearms several-fold. While the number of calibers possible to suppress with this system is far reaching, always contact the suppressor manufacturer prior to using it with any caliber other than that specifically listed. The tiny 4.75-inch barrel makes a fantastic platform for the M.I.M.S. suppressor, as you get the benefit of a suppressor with a huge amount of volume with the benefit of a useful overall length. The suppressor only protrudes 5.5 inches beyond the end of the POF-USA P-9x rail system.

The MGI Military MARCK-15 Modular Lower Receiver seemed like a logical choice to use with this system given the ability to use a mag-well built specifically for the magazine we needed to use with this upper receiver. When combined with their 9mm SMG mag-well the owner can utilize factory Colt 9mm magazines and slightly modified Uzi magazines with no adapters or modifications. The correct magazine for the caliber and the correct magazine for the upper receiver will always assist in enhancing performance variables no longer necessary. The more adapters or custom magazines that are necessary can hinder the performance of a system greatly, and the MGI Lower, the correct magazine and the correct upper receiver came together to function as intended.

Not only can this writer recommend the Coastal/MGI 9mm system to the readers of Small Arms Review magazine, he will be adding this system to his collection at his own expense.

	Bullet Weight	Bullet Type	Extreme Speed	High/Low	Average MV	5-shot Group
SBR Green Match	90 Grain	Frangible	30 fps	1,240 fps 1,210 fps	1,226 fps	3.250 in
Winchester (white box)	115 Grain	FMJ	48 fps	1,229 fps 1,181 fps	1,202 fps	3.759 in
Wolf Performance Ammo	115 Grain	FMJ	27 fps	1,139 fps 1,111 fps	1,120 fps	3.627 in
Winchester Subsonic	147 Grain	JHP	77 fps	1,040 fps 963 fps	999 fps	1,935 in
Atlanta Arms Subsonic	147 Grain	JHP	26 fps	917 fps 891 fps	905 fps	2.464 in

Measurements recorded 7/29/09. Temperature 79 F. Elevation at range is 310' above sea level. MV testing recorded on PACT MKIV XP Championship Chronograph and Timer from a distance of 8' in front of suppressor. Accuracy testing consisted of 5-shot groups fired from 50 yards with 9x mil-dot scope.

The CAV-15 from Cavalry Arms

Sgt. Time Drake, USMC, test fires the CAV-15 to compare the feel against his issue M16A2 he uses in competition on his rifle team.

I have written several times that the M-16/AR-15 is my favorite weapons system, and given the opportunity to test a new innovation in this area, I gladly accepted. I have tried several parts and accessories for these firearms in the past. Some of them have been pretty complicated and difficult to install. Others are quite simple but still give the rifle system another "push" in becoming even better and more versatile. Almost all of these new parts and accessories I have tested have been somewhat useful in aiding function, reliability and accuracy over the original design.

Many of the latest AR-15 design changes have been caliber conversions ranging from the modest .22 long rifle cartridge to a few of the massive .50 cal rounds on the market today. Sworn at by some and sworn by, by others, I have enjoyed most of what has crossed my path. This current shooting endeavor is just as far from the traditional AR-15 family guns as the caliber swaps.

This latest product I had the pleasure to test is closer to an evolution of the weapons system than it is an upgrade or an accessory. The CAV-15 is much different than any other firearm I have tested in this family. The CAV-15 lower receiver incorporates an integral pistol grip and shoulder stock and all has been injected molded from Glass-Filled Nylon 6 Polymer. The receiver is actually molded in two pieces, then sonic welded and bolted together in a clamshell fashion. Before it is shipped, it can be completely assembled if you choose, including the lower receiver small parts, buffer tube, buffer, buffer spring and butt plate. Once you receive your CAV-15 lower receiver assembled in this fashion, all you will need is the upper receiver with the bolt and carrier as well as the buffer and buffer spring to be finished. You can also purchase it "stripped" and it will only include the integral pistol grip, butt stock, buffer tube and butt plate with trap door. In the "stripped" option you will need to obtain a lower receiver parts kit containing the hammer, trigger, push pins, etc.

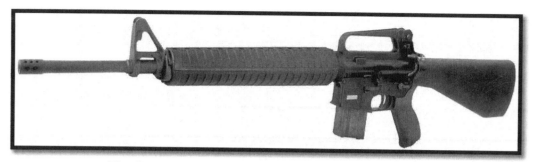

The CAV-15 is light, rugged, and comfortable to shoot.

In passing the rifle for the first time to friends and other fans of the Black Rifle, the immediate response is always the same. They pick it up, and lower and raise it a few times. With a confused look on their face they will tap the magazine well and flip it over to look at the markings. Absolutely everyone I have shown the CAV-15 to has looked at me and said "It's Plastic". Then they place it to their shoulder and start to smile. The CAV-15 stock is a full 1" longer than a standard AR-15A2 and fits most shooters very well.

The polymer used to manufacture the CAV-15 is very strong and extremely resistant to corrosion. (When is the last time you saw rusty plastic?) The CAV-15 receiver is manufactured to the same specifications as the aluminum counterparts on the market, utilizing all the standard lower receiver parts and pins. This rugged receiver and stock set provides a quality and strength equal or superior to several of the traditional aluminum receivers, all while shaving almost 3/4 of a pound off the weight of a standard aluminum lower with standard stock and pistol grip.

The receiver, pistol grip, and stock are actually molded in two pieces, then sonic welded and bolted together.

The first thing that came to my mind when I first saw a CAV-15 was "why plastic"? In speaking with Shawn Nealon, the proprietor, it became very obvious. Shawn comes from a family background rich in plastics manufacturing. As a young man Shawn worked for the family plastic business and had

124

envisioned making a Nylon AR-15 in his early years. Where it was so far from the business's typical product line the idea was rejected but Shawn never forgot his proposal. His business was in the field of plastics but his interest was in the field of firearms and it was only a few short years ago that these fields would intersect.

The idea of a "plastic rifle" is really nothing completely new. In the early 70's Colt toyed with the idea a little and even built a prototype. It is believed that it never went forward because a plastic gun was considered undesirable and almost unmarketable. As proof to this school of thought, think of all the naysayers who have condemned the AR-15/M16 and have referred to it negatively as a "plastic rifle" as it is. They said the same about the Glock pistols....

The manufacturing process for the CAV-15 is well suited to adopt various colors. Cavalry Arms offers these receivers, along with a matching handguard, in black, green, gray, tan, blue and even yellow. Nothing will get you a funny look from traditional shooters at the range like a yellow rifle with a big magazine.

For the purposes of testing the CAV-15, I used a J&T Distributing "Expedition" Upper Receiver. These are quality, barreled receivers available directly from J&T Distributing of Winchester Kentucky. These barreled upper receivers utilize a match grade barrel with an integral muzzle brake in order to be legal for "post-ban" rifle applications. Note: Since receiving the CAV-15 receiver for testing, Cavalry Arms has started offering complete rifles, as well as the option of purchasing just the receiver with integral pistol grip and stock.

The first and most apparent difference when shouldering the CAV-15 at the shooting range for the first time is the additional length of the stock. It feels very comfortable for the shooter. Upon firing the first couple of rounds there was an obvious "dry spring" sound coming from the stock. The bolt carrier was sliding back into the buffer tube fairly slowly as well, and a small application of lubrication seemed to correct both of these concerns in short order.

The magazine well was a little tighter than many of the traditional, aluminum AR-15 receivers I have assembled and fired in the past. It was not tight enough to hinder operation of the firearm but it was noticeably tighter than I am used to, and completely eliminated any side-to-side or front-to-back movement of the magazine while locked in the well. It was not so tight as to prohibit dropping the magazine at the push of the magazine release however. Very nice. The magazine well is also beveled to assist the shooter in inserting the magazine effortlessly.

The CAV-15 on the left compared to a standard M16A2 on right. The beveled magazine well of the CAV-15 makes fast mag changes a snap.

The pins in the lower receiver that push through and lock onto the lugs of the upper receiver pushed through the lugs very hard. The fit between the upper receiver and lower receiver was very positive and had absolutely no side-to-side "slop". I have only had a few upper/lower receiver combinations this snug in the past and for all others I have installed an ACCU-wedge(tm) to tighten the fit. The advantage of this tight fit is the obvious gain in accuracy due to the elimination of movement between the receivers. The only downfall of the relationship of the receivers remaining so tight is the time it takes to push or pull the pins out when you desire to clean the rifle of to swap upper receivers to another configuration increased. Personally I will opt for the accuracy.

The lettering on the side of the lower receiver is molded right into the receiver during the manufacturing process. The serial number is on a small metal plate attached to the lower receiver directly below the markings, in its usual position.

The pricing of the CAV-15 rifles is quite attractive. The stripped receivers have a suggested retail of $150.00 for green or black. Tan or gray retail at $170.00 and you can have one in blue or yellow for $190.00. Add $100.00 for complete lower receivers including the parts outlined above. Complete rifles start at $650.00. Several options and accessories are available as well as various configurations.

I like the CAV-15 and I think it is a nice addition to the collection of any black rifle fan. If you do a little hunting with .223 you will enjoy the reduction in weight, and many of you will like the longer stock. If you have shorter arms, you can utilize the option of having the stock shortened. In speaking with Shawn just before press time, it seems they are considering shortening the rifle back to a standard A1 length in the next year or so because the demand for the shorter rifle is so great. We will keep you posted.

The STAR-15 from DoubleStar Corporation

There is a new kid on the block in the arena of manufacturing AR-15/M16 type rifle systems and that new kid already has years of experience.

DoubleStar Corporation is the latest venture of the Starnes family from Winchester Kentucky. You may recognize the Starnes name as Jack and Teresa Starnes have been in business selling AR-15/M16 parts and accessories for over 25 years doing business as J&T Distributing. They were formally known as J&T Surplus. They can be found regularly at several large gun shows nationwide including Knob Creek, SHOT Show, SAR Show in Phoenix, Arizona and the NRA Convention. This latest venture brings another generation of the Starnes family into the family business with the addition of Jesse as the new Vice President of DoubleStar Corp. Jesse has several years in this type of business as well due to his involvement in J&T. Teresa is currently the President of DoubleStar Arms and to the best of my knowledge DoubleStar is the only woman-owned military rifle manufacturer in the USA.

The primary difference between J&T Distributing and DoubleStar Corp. is that DoubleStar is manufacturing complete firearms and J&T sells only parts and accessories. Even though they remain closely related, the two businesses are completely separate.

I received the first test example in a flat top, STARCAR carbine configuration. The lack of a sighting system was quickly corrected by adding a C-More Tactical Sight. The second test example is a standard Dissipator version with the optional ported barrel.

I am pleased to report that I was not dissatisfied with either rifle. The flat top carbine is extremely comfortable to shoot with the addition of the C-More Tactical Sight. The low sight height permits a low cheek weld that is repeatable in the same position for use of the iron sights, a red dot sight or both. The C-More Tactical Sight is designed to mount right on the receiver of the flat top and adds an A2 rear sight back to the rifle. With this system you can sight in the iron sights by looking through the glass where the red dot appears. It is best used in conjunction with the red dot but always remains an available backup should something electronically fail.

The Dissipator is a design that caught my eye several years ago but for some reason I never had the opportunity to fire one. The Dissipator was designed to utilize a short carbine gas system and barrel, but adapted to fit under full-length handgards. This leaves very little barrel extending past the front sight post and has a great look to it. The look is of the full-length rifle but the feel is very well balanced and swings around easier than expected, especially in tight quarters because it is still the short length of the carbine. This is a big plus when the shooter does not require or desire the full-length of the standard rifle barrel and this system gets a big, long anticipated "thumbs up" from me. Another plus of the Dissipator is that the full-length handguard allows for better control than the short handguard and the shooter also has the benefit of the long sight radius that the A2 sighting system was designed to provide.

Star-15 Dissipator on top and STARCAR on bottom. This particular STARCAR is a flat top and I added a C-More Tactical Sight for shooting.

The range time proved both rifles to be extremely accurate and reliable. Our test ammo was standard SS-109 62-grain ammunition and performed well in both configurations. Both barrels feature a rate of twist of one turn in 9 inches. All the shooting was done from a bench and the Dissipator was fired only utilizing the standard A2 open sights.

As for reliability, the only failure to feed or extract happened when I inadvertently inserted an out-of-spec magazine I had previously marked for the parts pile into the Dissipator and it would not perform. A quick examination proved the bad magazine to be the problem as suspected and it was corrected immediately upon changing magazines.

The fit and finish of both rifles was tight and even. A moderate amount of pressure was required to remove the upper and lower receiver retaining pin and this indicates the close tolerances required to maximize accuracy potential. The finish was dark and even and consistent with all upper and lower receivers.

DoubleStar Corporation is offering several new variations of the Star-15 rifle system not currently found elsewhere on the market. While the product line includes everything from standard rifles to match rifles there are also a few innovations exclusive to DoubleStar. One of their popular new rifle systems is the CritterSlayer. It incorporates a 24-inch fluted, super match barrel and full-floating Badger trapezoidal handguards. Another of their exclusive rifles is the Star-15 Lightweight Tactical. It utilizes a fluted heavy barrel and the upper is 11.2 ounces lighter than a standard heavy barreled upper. The stock looks like a standard A2 stock except that it is 3.375 inches shorter and was designed for comfortable use while wearing body armor. When dealing with DoubleStar Corporation you are not limited to just a small number of standard models and configurations. At last count they were offering almost 300 variations of their rifles.

The new rifle line by DoubleStar should certainly go places fast. With the experience of J&T Distributing in the accessory field for so many years and listening to what customers wanted and specifically look for in these weapon systems they are poised to fill any void they can discover in this extremely competitive market.

Star-15 Specifications STARCAR Carbine and Dissipator	
Caliber:	5.56x45 mm NATO
Overall Length:	34.25" (869.95 mm)
Barrel Length:	16" (406.40 mm)
Pitch of Rifling:	One turn in 9" (1/228 mm)
Twist of Rifling:	Right Hand / Six-Groove
Method of Operation:	Gas
Lockup Method:	Rotating multi-lug bolt
Front Sight:	Protected Post
Rear Sight:	Protected Peep
Weight:	7.1 pounds for STARCAR (3.22 kg); 7.5

	pounds for Dissipator (3.42 kg)
Weight of Magazine:	1 pound 30-round, loaded (.453 kg)
Receiver Material:	Forged 7075-T6 Aluminum
Retail Pricing:	$774.95 STARCAR (Basic); $874.95 Dissipator (Basic); Several upgrades available for additional fee

The Dalphon .50 AE AR-15 Conversion

Without a doubt, my favorite rifle is the AR-15. It is arguable that there are many others that perform better for specific tasks, but for an all-around gun this brainchild of Eugene Stoner is a hard choice to beat. The number of new caliber conversions manufactured by Dalphon now opens the spectrum even more.

I have enjoyed the versatility of the AR family of rifles for many years. The number of configurations possible have always been limited only to one's imagination. My first one was an original Colt SP-1 with a pencil barrel and beavertail hand-guards. I stopped at a local gun shop with my buddy Tim and he looked it over for me. He started pushing pins and pulling parts, and eventually gave it the stamp of approval. He gave me a crash course in operation, care and maintenance, and the rest is now history.

Before this purchase, most of my firearms were more "traditional". I grew up in the "gun culture" being surrounded with firearms of all sorts, but the vast majority were hunting rifles or target pistols. I always had an admiration for firearms and learned to shoot in the days before I was old enough to remember. My first exposure to "military style firearms" was when my father purchased a Bushmaster Pistol manufactured by Gwinn Firearms back in the late 70's. I think this was my first true love. I wasn't allowed to shoot it right away but I always knew I wanted to. Until that point I was only regularly exposed to firearms where it was common to fire 20 rounds or so, give it a cleaning and retire it until the next trip to the range. With this new addition came the necessity for big magazines and more ammo. This would prove to be the beginning of a lifelong hobby, and the basis for many future career choices. I know I have said it many times before, but once again, "Thanks Dad."

In my early days collecting the AR-15 rifles, there were not many caliber conversions being marketed that I was aware of. They were almost all chambered for .223 (5.56x45) with a few 9x19 examples out there. The latter were fairly rare and definitely more expensive. Colt had a .22 Long Rifle sub-caliber unit, and Jon Ciener was marketing the Atchisson kit, but I was never really interested in stepping down in ballistic properties. The original Armalite AR-10's in .308 (7.62x51) were very rare and expensive and were never a realistic option.

In order to satisfy my desire to study and collect these rifles, I was on a mission to buy every part for every configuration I could find. That poor SP-1 sported almost every stock on the market and the barrel lengths covered all the bases as well. The hand-guards varied from the original beavertails, to the A2 Style round ones, the carbine A2 style on the shorty upper and even sported the M-203 hand-guards when a flare launcher was added to the family. After a while it was just obvious that a new caliber was all that was left.

Close-up of the modified bolt face.

My quest was a lonely one without many options, but to anyone on this same road today Dalphon Manufacturing is here to assist you. I first met the folks at Dalphon at the Soldier of Fortune Convention a few years back. They had some pretty innovative products on display. I noticed their suppressors first, and after walking past their display a few times I noticed that the bore on a few of their AR barrels was a little "large". I believe it was a 9mm upper I was looking at, but they had many more in the works. They have an impressive product line and the AR-15 caliber conversions are just a part of their business.

When they introduced their newest upper receiver chambered in .50 Action Express it caught my attention right away. I seem to have this foolish grin that washes over my face whenever I encounter a firearm with a bore of 1/2" or better and it was definitely present again this time. Someone had tried this conversion a few years back and it kind of drifted into the shadows but remained an interest of mine nonetheless. I remember reading about the massive muzzle energy and stopping power, and thinking it should be on my list to someday own one. I contacted Dalphon and they shipped a unit right out.

While waiting for it to come in, I did a little homework on available ammo. Back when the .50AE round was first introduced, it was as expensive as .50 BMG. If we could find it at $1.50 per round it was a good deal. I was pretty impressed this time when I picked up a few boxes of Speer Gold Dot for less than $1.00 per round. There are also many ammunition choices now, as where there were only two originally.

Since I also knew ahead of time that it would arrive in a "flat-top" configuration I started looking around for a suitable test scope. I contacted C-More Systems and they shipped me one of their Tactical Sights. This seemed to be a natural marriage, and when it arrived and was mounted, my suspicions were confirmed. It was perfect for the Dalphon unit.

When the gun arrived, I took it apart to see what made it tick. The most noticeable difference from a standard AR-15 was the barrel assembly. It is a heavy 16" stainless steel bull barrel surrounded by a round hand-guard. It is gas operated and utilizes a unique adjustable gas block. The gas block is moved forward or rearward to adjust gas pressure. There are 4 Allen screws that must be loosened and re-tightened when the block is in its desired position. There are currently 2 settings, one for hot ammo and one for regular loads, and it is my understanding that a fully adjustable gas system is in the development stages.

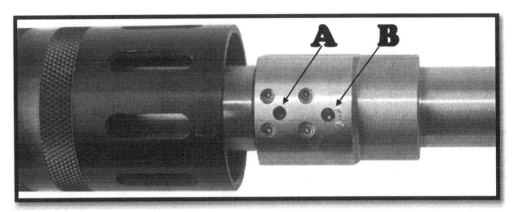

The indicated holes are the settings for the adjustable gas block. If the first hole (A) is centered, it is in the "Standard Ammo" setting. If the second hole (B) is centered it is in the "Hot Ammo" setting. The other four visible holes are the allen screws that hold the gas block in place.

Some of the .50 AE ammo on the market creates much more pressure than other brands and this has made it necessary to bleed off a little gas to prevent damage to the firearm. Most often the extractor would be the victim of these hot loads and the easing of the gas pressure has evidently corrected the situation. IMI Ammunition is commonly a little hotter than many other commercial brands and the hot setting is actually stamped IMI.

I had done enough fondling and it was time to test it out. I mounted the C-More Sight and it surprisingly set almost dead center from the factory. The detail and quality of the C-More was amazing. Not only was it very functional and comfortable, but the aesthetics were incredible. They incorporate an E2 style "rear sight" into their design that looks just like a factory Colt unit. Everyone who examined the scope thought the "rear sight" portion of the scope was part of the rifle itself. The C-More Tactical Sight is a red-dot sight that also utilizes the iron sight for superior accuracy. Having used a number of red-dot sights over the years, and seeing few real improvements, I set my expectations low. I am pleased to report here that I was not disappointed, but actually very impressed with this system. Target acquisition is fast, and by using the dot in conjunction with the rear sight it is much more consistent than any I have used in the past. Thumbs up to C-More.

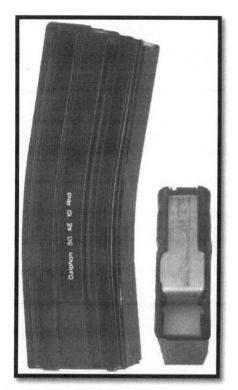

While the magazine body is unmodified, the follower is new, and a spacer / feed ramp was added to accommodate the shorter round.

Due to all the stories I had heard about this particular caliber being fired in a 16" barrel as opposed to the much shorter barrel of the Desert Eagle pistol, I wanted to run it through a chronograph and alleviate some fact from a little fiction right away. We set up a Dillon chronograph and I loaded a magazine with Speer 325 grain Gold Dots. We wanted a string of five rounds to get an average reading. As soon as I squeezed the trigger the first time I knew this was not your typical AR. The average bullet speed was over 1,760 feet per second, and the recoil was very noticeable.

I had expectations of light to moderate recoil due to the very efficient buffer system, but these expectations were soon quelled. This bad boy has some thump! Now don't get me wrong, it is not anywhere near severe enough to discourage you from shooting it again (and again...and again...), but you definitely know it is there. The sound is moderate, and the heavy barrel assists you in keeping the muzzle down a little bit when firing rounds close together.

There was a private shoot that would be attended by many seasoned Emma-gees coming up and I thought it would be the perfect place to get the "man-on-the-street" opinion of the Dalphon conversion. This was a shoot for the members of the Hiram Maxim group that work at the big Military Firearms Shoot & Expo every year, and was an opportunity for the crew to get a little shooting in. I had mentioned to a few of the guys that I may be bringing the Dalphon and when I pulled in I was asked right away of its whereabouts. When I pulled it out and started loading a magazine, an instant line began to form. When I set the rifle down and the bore diameter was visible, the line got longer.

I gave everyone interested a few rounds to fire at the appliance or automobile of their choice, and almost all the reactions were the same. After firing a couple rounds, they would typically rotate their shoulder or make some type of signal that they were aware of the recoil, and a big smile would wash over their face. When the line would quiet down, the first question I would get was "How much are these?"

When asked about their opinion of this combo everyone liked the C-More Tactical Sight, and all were

Left to right: .25ACP, 9x19, .45ACP, .50AE.

intrigued by the massive bore of the rifle. When I asked about the recoil, almost everyone compared it to shooting a shotgun, and no one thought it was too excessive. The unanimous decision was it was certainly different than any other AR-15 family rifle they had ever encountered and all liked it.

I was very impressed with the quality and the craftsmanship of the Dalphon system. The unit functioned almost flawlessly. The only stoppage I encountered was a short cycle due to the fact that I started out with the gas system in the hot ammo setting when it was not necessary. I returned the gas block to the correct position and it continued to function great.

The finish on the upper receiver as well as the Dalphon lower receiver I tested it on was nice and dark. It was not shiny at all, and actually resembled a very desirable, early Colt finish. I have seen many different colored receivers in the past, that seemed to cover the spectrum from gray, to purple, to gloss black and this is definitely one of the best finishes I have encountered.

The necessary modifications to the bolt and the magazine were very professionally done and it is obvious that Dalphon did a lot of R&D before marketing this conversion. The bolt was opened up to accommodate the much larger base of the .50AE round and the extractor also needed to be modified. Specially modified extractors are available for your spare parts kits.

The magazine utilizes a standard 30-round magazine body with a modified follower and a built in spacer / feed ramp to accommodate the shorter cartridge. I experienced no malfunctions due to the design of the magazine. Just like the remainder of the conversion, it was very well made.

The bolt carrier and lower receiver remain original and unmodified. For some of you this statement may be the answer to a burning question you have had all along. Without a doubt, the most commonly asked question I have encountered with this conversion was not "How is the recoil?" but rather "Can you shoot it in full auto on a registered lower?" Well, yes Virginia, there is a Santa Claus, and yes, now you can shoot the massive .50 Action Express in full auto.

Dalphon is currently manufacturing upper receivers in 45ACP, 40S&W, 9mm, 10mm and 7.62x39. Others coming soon include 44 Mag, 440 Corbon and 357. If the quality of their .50AE upper receiver is a reflection of the quality of these others, I am sure you will be impressed.

DPMS Panther Arms LR-.308

The AR-15 Rifle System Returns To Its Roots

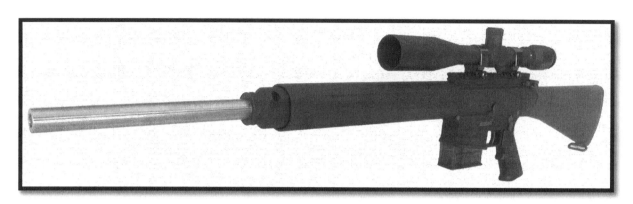

Many newcomers to the world of military firearms are excited about what seems to be the latest craze in AR-15 caliber conversions. We have seen many pistol caliber conversions and special offerings over the years, from .50AE and even .50 BMG single-shot upper receivers, all the way down to dedicated .22LR systems. The major focus now, seems to be with many major manufacturers who are offering a variant of this rifle in 7.62x51mm (.308 NATO). Well, this latest offering may be an interesting one, but there is certainly nothing new about this rifle and caliber combination.

The roots of the M16/AR-15 rifle system can be traced back to this caliber in its very early stages of development. Information on the original AR-10 designates that the first Stoner design in 1953 was originally chambered in 30-06 and was soon modified to 7.62 NATO because of the increasing popularity of the cartridge. Over a period of several years, the AR-10 eventually led to the AR-15, chambered in the now popular 5.56x45mm cartridge, after going through a series of lesser-known and short-lived model and caliber designations.

Incorporated in 1986, DPMS (Defense Procurement Manufacturing Services, Inc.) was originally a Department of Defense consulting agency. They now manufacture precision Mil-Spec and commercial parts and offer an enormous line of AR-15 type rifles for civilian, law-enforcement and military use. They have been manufacturing their .308 line of rifles for approximately 2 years.

The DPMS rifle line is as diverse as the imagination of the end user. Starting with their standard .223 Panther Carbine, they cover all the traditional configurations you would expect to encounter, in several barrel lengths and styles. The inventory really starts to look different from most AR-15/M16 manufacturers once you get past these more traditional models. Where they really stand out is in their specialty line of rifles. Their Panther Race Gun and Arctic Panther look as though they slid out of a futuristic Sci-Fi movie. These are serious precision rifles that offer such options as CRYO barrel treatment and Titanium Nitrate coated bolt carrier assemblies. To cater to the southpaws, a left-handed version of many of their rifles is available in their product line. For law enforcement agencies and qualified individuals, they offer their Panther Kitty-Kat, which is a .223 variant of the M16 with a 7-inch barrel.

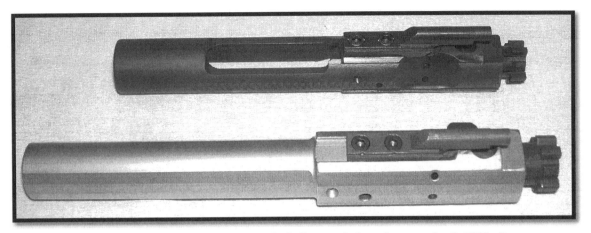

The massive DPMS .308 NATO bolt (bottom) dwarfs a standard .223 bolt.

The .308 caliber rifles are currently available in 3 configurations. The Panther Long Range .308 utilizes a 24-inch, 416 Stainless steel bull barrel. The Panther Long Range .308B is equipped with an 18-inch, 4140 Chrome-moly steel bull barrel. The last is the Panther Long Range .308T, and it is standard with a 16-inch 4140 Chrome-moly steel heavy barrel. All barrels are free floating and all .308 series upper receivers are "flat-tops" with a 7-inch, MIL-STD-1913 rail for mounting optics. At this time no iron sights are available for the .308 rifle line. By the time you receive this issue of Small Arms Review there will be many more configurations of the .308 rifles available. Plans are in the works for collapsible stocks, carbine barrels and even select-fire variants for law enforcement agencies and qualified individuals. Additionally, there will be detachable carry handles and A2 style upper receivers as well as threaded barrels with original style flash hiders in the near future.

The rifle provided to Small Arms Review for testing was the Panther Long Range .308. The first thing that immediately caused this rifle to stand apart from all other AR-15 type rifles the author has handled, was the 24-inch stainless bull barrel. An outside diameter of almost 1-inch (.920 to be exact) combined with the bright, stainless finish of the 9 1/2 inches of barrel that was exposed past the handguards and the gas block makes this rifle immediately distinguishable from others. The initial reaction of everyone who had handled it was the same, and that was that it looked heavy. Although the rifle weighs in at 11.28 pounds unloaded, it handles quite well and is not nearly as "front heavy" as you would initially suspect. The balancing point is actually only a little over an inch forward of the receiver when the rifle is unloaded.

The test rifle came equipped with a JP Enterprises, adjustable trigger system and provided a quick and clean break with no creep or excessive travel. JP Enterprises manufactures these trigger systems for most AR-15 type rifles and anyone who owns one would certainly find an immediate improvement in their grouping by installing one. These trigger systems are available from DPMS, Inc., and retail under $130.00.

To look at this rifle quickly, it shares almost all of the physical characteristics of the standard AR-15. This rifle, however, is far from being one of the standard "drop-on" caliber conversions we have become accustomed to. There is nothing that is compatible with the .223 series of rifles other than a few miscellaneous parts such as the pistol grip, magazine release, bolt-hold-open device and the trigger mechanism. Both the lower and upper receivers have been completely redesigned and everything has been enlarged a little to accommodate the larger round. The .223 cartridge is 45mm long, compared to the .308 being 51mm long, and a standard AR-15 magazine-well would not accommodate the additional length. This additional length also translates to a longer stroke in the action, in order to correctly eject a fired case and to pick up the next round from the magazine. Due to the necessity of a longer action, the bolt carrier has also been redesigned and the bolt is larger in diameter than a standard AR-15 bolt in order to safely function with the larger case diameter of the .308. The base of a standard .223 case is in the area of .375-inch where the .308 base measures almost .470-inch.

One of the most frequently asked questions I encounter when talking about this rifle is, "Will a DIAS or lightning link function in it?" The answer is no. Due to both the upper and lower receiver being completely redesigned, combined with the additional length of the bolt carrier, neither will physically work. It may also not be legal under ATF&E guidelines where this rifle was not the one intended for use with the DIAS or Lightning link.

Got Sights?

Since the Panther Long Range .308 is not equipped with iron sights, we needed something to set on top of it before we could do any shooting. It didn't make any sense to grab one of the several inexpensive pieces of glass lying around, because it wouldn't have done justice to the rifle. I contacted Barry at BW Optic and he was kind enough to send one of his scopes with the Y-TAC reticle for evaluation. We received a 2.5x10x42mm Tactical Scope. The BW Optic Y-TAC scope is custom manufactured by IOR Bucuresti in Bucurest, Romania. These scopes are manufactured using the finest German glass from Schott Glasswerk and feature the Carl Ziess T-3 lens coating system. IOR has been manufacturing optics since 1936 and currently has over 1,000 employees in 2 different plants in Bucurest. The author found the light transmission, clarity and resolution to be parallel with or superior to the nicest scopes he has ever handled.

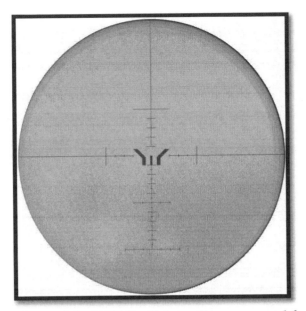

A photo of the Y-TAC reticle on the scope used for testing. The reticle is photo-engraved on the glass and functions as a rangefinder as well as an aiming mechanism.

The superior glass and workmanship were not the only apparent advantages of this scope. The unique Y-TAC reticle is quite different from most "traditional" sporting and military optics. The Y-TAC reticle was designed for optimum low-light performance as well as speed in ranging and target acquisition. The reticle looks similar to the iron sights on some pre-World War II rifles. In the sight picture, the "wings" of the front sight are on each side of the "post" from the rear sight, and both are incorporated in the reticle of this scope. The "post" is utilized for holding the point of aim, and sized at 0.9MOA at 100 yards; it is easy to pick up in all types of lighting. The "wings" portion of the reticle assist in ranging by allowing the shooter to instantly measure his target based on the known measurements of the B-27 target. The Y-TAC reticle is photo-engraved on the German glass. The tube is 30mm in diameter, and all BW Optic scopes are waterproof, dry Nitrogen filled and have a factory, lifetime warranty. The scope as tested has a MSRP of $769.00 and is available directly from BW Optic.

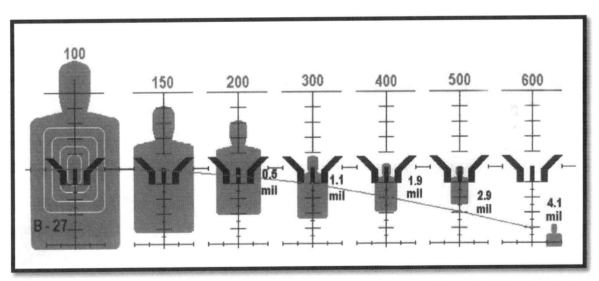

This illustration shows the Y-TAC reticle in relation to targets out to 600 yards. Using the "wings" portion of the reticle, the user can quickly range the target. As illustrated, using the "shoulders" in ranging will provide an upper body hit all the way out to 400 meters without moving the firearm. This trajectory chart is for an M16A2, 20" barrel with 62 grain .223 ammunition.

Range Time

Our time spent at the range with the DPMS Long Range .308 showed the impressive capabilities of this rifle system. The ammunition selected for this rifle testing was M118 Lake City Special Ball. A quick bore-sight got us on paper and we were shooting in the bull at 100 yards in no time. It was not uncommon to fire sub MOA groups at 100 yards with this rifle, scope and ammunition combination. The M118 Special Ball is a 173-grain boat tail that also performed extremely well at 200 yards. Without adjusting the elevation, the point of impact was approximately 1.5 inches below the hold, and the groups were still in the 1-inch range. Without making any adjustments, we fired a few groups with the new WOLF .308 Win. 150 grain FMJ ammunition. It functioned well in the rifle and was a much hotter load than the M118 Special Ball, evident by the increased ejection distance. We were pleasantly surprised at the grouping at 100 yards. The point of impact was actually the same and while the groups were not nearly as tight as with the M118 Special Ball ammo, we were still able to fire several groups well under 2 inches and one group around 1-inch. The drop at 200 yards was closer to 4 inches compared with the 1.5-inch drop with the M118 Special Ball. The third ammunition tested was a hunting load by Federal Cartridge Co. We fired a few groups with the Federal Premium 180 grain Nosler Partition ammunition, and once again, at 100 yards the point of impact was the same. Time after time, 3 shots would produce 3 bulls. These groups were all around 1-inch, but nothing as tight as the M118 ammunition. At 200 yards the Federal ammunition proved to hit approximately 2 inches below the point of aim and consistently shot in groups between 2 and 3 inches in diameter.

Summary

The DPMS Long Range .308 performs like many high-end bolt-action rifles but retains the advantage of the fast follow-up shot you can only get from a semiautomatic action. For any fan of the AR-15 rifle system there should be an immediate attraction. The quality and craftsmanship on the specimen we tested was flawless and it functioned great with all ammunition we fired. With a retail price of $1,149.00, I have certainly spent much more money on much less performance in the past. I can easily recommend the Panther Long Range .308 Rifle for any recreational shooter, competitor, hunter or professional operator, and know they will be impressed regardless of the application.

Panther Long Range .308 Specifications	
Caliber:	.308 Winchester (7.62x51 mm)
Overall Length:	43.6" (1107.44 mm)
Barrel Length:	24" (609.60 mm)
Weight, unloaded:	11.28 pounds (5.11 kg)
Method of Operation:	Gas operated rotating bolt; semiautomatic
Feed Mechanism:	5, 9, 10 or 20-round detachable magazine
Barrel:	416 Stainless steel, 6-groove, right handed twist, 1/10 twist. Button rifled.
Sights:	None. 7" MIL-STD 1913 rail for scope mounting
Finish:	Hard coat anodized per Mil Spec
Stock:	Standard A2 Mil Spec
Handguards:	Ribbed aluminum, free floating
MSRP:	$1,149.00

DPMS Panther Arms LR-308AP4

The DPMS LR-308AP4 as it was tested. Combined with high quality ammo, an Elite Iron silencer, and a BW Optic Y-TAC Scope, this 16" barreled, semiautomatic carbine performed well above our expectations.

From a distance it looks like another tricked-out M4-style black rifle. There is something a little different but it may take a second to put your finger on it unless you are a died-in-the-wool AR-15/M16 fan. While it looks like an M4 on steroids, there is no doubt it is a 7.62x51mm NATO powerhouse.

The original DPMS LR-308 was tested in Small Arms Review (Vol. 8, No. 5, February 2005) and was very well received so the bar was set high for this latest addition to the DPMS Panther Arms .308 line up. Originally tested with a 24-inch, Stainless Steel Heavy Barrel and A2 Mil Spec Stock, this newer AP-4 variant sports a much lighter, and shorter 16-inch barrel that is contoured similar to the original 5.56x45mm M4, and has a 6-position telescoping stock.

The lower receiver and bolt group are the same as the LR-308 with all the changes to the AP4 upgrade being in the upper receiver. The upper receiver is a thick-walled extrusion from 6066-T6 aluminum. It is hard anodized and Teflon coated black to perfectly match the LR-308 lower receiver. The shell deflector and forward assist unit are machined as a single unit. On top is an A3 style flat top allowing the use of several sighting options. The front sight is a standard A2 sight assembly and can be combined with several popular rear sighting or BUIS (Back Up Iron Sight) devices, and even used in conjunction with a plethora of low magnification, electronic sights.

Since we had a positive experience with the BW Optic Y-TAC scope the last time we tested the LR-308, it was decided to use it again in with new configuration. The BW Optic Y-TAC used in this article was a 2.5 to 10-power scope with a 42mm objective. These scopes are custom built by IOR Bucuresti in Bucharest, Romania. The photoengraved German glass used in the assembly of the Y-TAC features the Carl Ziess T-3 lens coating system and combined with the 30mm tube it provides an excellent sight, especially when multiple loads are to be used. With a scope of this nature it is easy to "zero" a specific load and have several different points of aim to use for specialty rounds and always be "on" without firing multiple test shots when in the field. We will get into a little more detail on multiple loads and point of aim vs. point of impact later in the article.

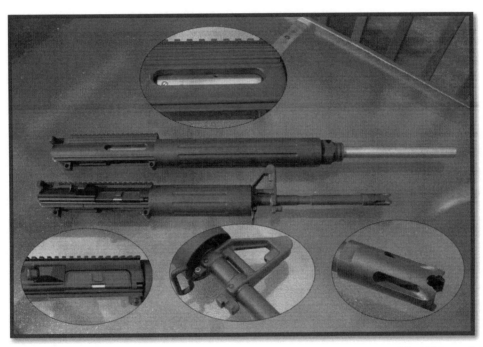

DPMS LR-308 upper with 24" heavy barrel above LR-308AP4 upper with 16" barrel. The lower receiver is the same for both rifles although the stock for the AP4 is a 6-position collapsible stock instead of a standard A@-styl3 stock.

The barrel of the AP4 may be shorter and the overall gun much lighter than the original LR-308 but don't be fooled into thinking the changes were made at the expense of the performance. The 16-inch 4140 Chrome-moly steel barrel is contained inside a free floating handguard and is still a button rifled, 6-groove, 1 in 10-inch twist. The shorter barrel is completed with 308 Panther flash hider, which is attached via a standard 5/8x24 thread. This last little detail brought immediate joy to the author who contacted suppressor manufacturer Elite Iron and immediately ordered their D30 silencer to test in conjunction with this rifle.

Dale and Kathy Poling of Elite Iron have been involved in the machine gun and suppressor industry for several years. Their latest suppressor line, including the D22 and D30, are made with 304 stainless steel tubes and all internals are CNC machined from solid billet stainless steel. Upon assembly they are welded for added strength and durability. They can immediately be identified by their signature-knurled bands at the rifle end of the suppressor. Throughout our testing, the DPMS LR-308AP4 and the Elite Iron D30 silencer proved to be an excellent combination.

Range Time

Time at the range was spent with several types of ammunition. Other than a few failures to feed due to a damaged magazine (which was quickly identified and discarded) the function of the LR-308AP4 was excellent and uneventful. We used Wolf 150-grain FMJ, 173-grain M118 Lake City Special Ball and 168-grain Federal Gold Medal. While all functioned well and performed satisfactorily, the combination of the DPMS LR-308AP4, fitted with the Elite Iron D30 Silencer and loaded with the Federal Gold Medal ammo provided most excellent results.

When changing muzzle devices the point of impact is almost always affected and we wanted to measure this effect with a single type of ammo for maximum continuity. After shooting a few groups we chose the Federal Gold Medal to continue recording and we started measuring group size and point of impact shift. We first sighted the rifle in with no muzzle device. We reinstalled the factory Panther flash hider and shot a 5-shot group at 100 yards. It measured 1.56 inches and was centered 2.8 inches low and left of the point of aim (in the 7 o'clock position). We were thinking that 1.5 MOA was pretty impressive for a 16-inch barreled, semiautomatic rifle fired in a semi-rapid manor but things were about to get better. The second group we fired was done without any muzzle device and we again shot a 5-shot group at 100 yards. The point of impact was exactly the point of aim and the group measured an impressive 1.10 inches. Things just continued to get better. The Elite Iron D30 Silencer was attached and we fired a third 5-shot group. This time the point of impact shifted 3 inches to the right of the point of aim (in the 3 o'clock position) and measured an amazing .765 inches. Since we were shooting 5-shot groups we were impressed with this combination and continued to shoot the same point of impact for the remainder of the afternoon.

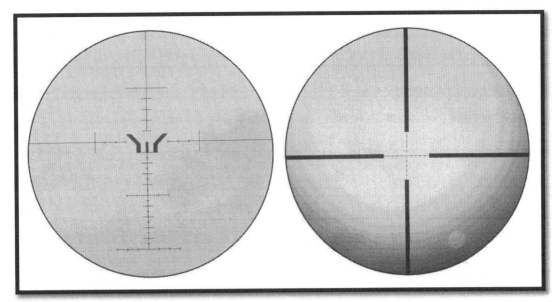

On the left is a photograph taken through the BW Optic Y-TAC scope tested on the DPMS-LR308AP4. The "Y" reticle is used as a range finder and the series of lines act to give the shooter multiple points of aim for different distances or types of ammunition. On the right is a photograph looking through the authors Leupold M8 Tactical Scope. The Mil-Dot reticle inside the heavy cross hairs is also one of the authors favorite patterns for using multiple types of ammunition or for shooting various distances.

Point of Impact vs. Point of Aim

Since it was brought up earlier, a little more should be said about this effect. Contrary to some beliefs, almost anything you do with a firearm in relation to the barrel can affect the point of impact. In the field of precision shooting there are several factors that determine exactly where the bullet is going to impact once the trigger is squeezed. Most are related to the shooter but even after the human factor is taken out there are many more forces at play. The harmonics and whip of the barrel change every time an accessory is added or removed. Most are sensitive enough that even the use of a bipod placed directly on the barrel instead of the stock can have a dramatic effect on accuracy. At times, removing and replacing the same accessories without tightening them the same can even show a slight difference in the group size or placement. Typically the whip effect of a barrel is more exaggerated or pronounced if the barrel is a long or thin barrel (or a combination of both) and lessened with a short and fat barrel, hence the popularity of "bull" barrels with serious target shooters.

Even though barrels tend to react differently to dissimilar stocks, loads or muzzle devices, they usually have some amazing continuity if those factors are not disrupted. That being said, once a firearm is setup the way the shooter wants to use it, leaving it alone is the best cure. When an accessory is added and the point of impact has shifted, all the shooter needs to do is re-zero the firearm with the new combination of parts. A look at the combination of the LR-308AP4 and the Elite Iron D30 Silencer is an excellent example of a situation when the performance can actually be improved. The group size was almost reduced by one half, dropping from 1.5 inches to almost 3/4 of an inch, consistently. All that was necessary was a re-zero of approximately 3 inches to the left and this mighty carbine was transformed into an extremely quiet, sub-MOA powerhouse. To be sure of your sighting, just make sure that every time changes are made to any portion of the system, recheck the zero.

Just before going to press we were informed by Dale Poling at Elite Iron that he has developed a system of "tuning" a rifle and suppressor so POI shift will be minimal, if measurable at all. According to Poling, using his method, if there is any POI shift it tends to be minimally vertical with no apparent horizontal shift at all. For more information on this latest finding you can contact Dale directly via e-mail at: Kpoling@Blackfoot.net

Point of impact is obviously also affected by the ammo you are using. Just like the examples explained above, a different load can produce as tight a group as the first, but if it isn't hitting the intended area it has little value to the shooter. One example where 2 different loads may be advantageous to a shooter would be when utilizing subsonic ammo for specialty applications and finding it necessary to also use high velocity ammo for other situations. During some earlier testing with subsonic ammunition for Small Arms Review (Vol. 9, No 9, June 2006) we fired a substantial amount of Engel Ballistic Research 7.62x51mm Thumper. This 180-grain projectile traveling at an average of 958 feet per second would consistently (and silently) impact the target at 6 inches below the point of aim established for the full strength projectile traveling at 2,642 feet per second. The windage was not affected at all. With the sound reduction being a big factor in some instances and the consistency being so tight, all the shooter has to do is choose a mil-dot with a 6-inch rise as the point of aim for use with the subsonic ammo, and aim directly at the target. When it becomes desirable to use the high velocity ammo again, the shooter just returns to using the original point of aim. The BW Optic Y-TAC is an excellent choice for an application such as this. The Leupold M8 Tactical Mil-Dot scope also works quite well for multi-load uses. With a little practice and an understanding of your firearm and ammo, it is amazingly simple and effective.

Summary

Even though the LR-308AP4 with the 16-inch barrel is much smaller and lighter than the original LR-308 with the 24-inch bull barrel, the performance is still extremely impressive. The threaded muzzle allows for the use of many accessories and the AP4 returns more traditional cosmetic features that some black rifle enthusiasts find desirable. The available telescopic stock allows for a smaller package when carrying or transporting and has a similar feel to the original M4. Based on the original Arma-Lite AR10 design, there are several magazines available in a number of materials and capacities, and they are reliable and inexpensive. Being a life-long fan of the black rifle as well as a student of the "School of Bigger is Better," this writer thoroughly enjoyed testing the LR-308AP4. Combined with the Elite Iron D30 Silencer it well surpassed any preconceived accuracy expectations and the combination is destined to become permanent fixtures in the Small Arms Research reference collection. With a suggested retail of $1,254, this rugged and well-built carbine is sure to make an excellent addition to the collection or any black rifle enthusiast.

Panther LR- .308 AP4 Specifications	
Caliber:	.308 Winchester (7.62x51 mm)
Overall Length:	39" (990.60 mm)
Barrel Length:	16" (406.40 mm)
Weight, unloaded:	8.5 pounds (3.85 kg)
Method of Operation:	Gas operated rotating bolt; semiautomatic
Feed Mechanism:	5, 9, 10 or 19-round detachable magazine
Barrel Twist:	6-groove, right handed twist, 1/10 twist
Sights:	Standard A2 Front Sight Assembly
Finish:	Hard coat anodized per Mil Spec
Stock:	AP4, 6-position telescoping stock
Handguards:	Carbine length free floating aluminum
MSRP:	$1,254

The P-308 SBR from POF-USA:
A Powerhouse in a PDW-size Package

Full left-side view of the POF-USA P-308. This .308 powerhouse is small enough to be used in tight quarters but still provides the ability to be effective at long distances if necessary.

Chambering the Black Rifle in .308 Win. (7.62x51mm NATO) is anything but a new idea. From the early ArmaLites to the current selection of workhorse rifles on the market today, this caliber has fared well in giving the end user the extra knock-down power at extended ranges while keeping the feel, fit and function of America's primary service rifle for well over 40 years. As mission objectives change we must adapt to the new tasks at hand, and welcome the addition of POF-USA's C.R.O.S. (Corrosion Resistant Operating System) technology with this combat proven caliber.

We have explored the POF-USA family of black rifles in past issues of SAR and have put them through some very heavy endurance testing. All have outperformed the claims by the manufacturer and the innovation in the weapon systems continues to evolve at an amazing pace. The latest rifle in the POF-USA product line is the P-308, a larger 7.62x51mm version of their P-415 weapon system. It combines the larger caliber of the early AR-10, Knight SR-25, DPMS LR-308, Remington R-25, and others, with the piston driven operating system used in the POF rifle family.

Upgrades and Options

A quick glance at the P-308 we are testing may look like a shortened version of any of the aforementioned rifles but it takes a close look to reveal some of the details that make the P-308 stand out.

- The 12.5-inch barrel is fluted to increase surface area for strength and cooling.

- The POF barrel nut is several times the size of a standard barrel nut and is made of Aluminum with the intended purpose of quickly drawing heat from the chamber and barrel at a faster rate without any meaningful additional weight gain.

- The new upper receiver and rail mechanism have been integrated into the latest version of what used to be referred to as the Predator Rail System. This latest design, the Modular Railed Receiver (MRR) extends completely over the gas block to the area above the charging handle providing a long, continuous Mil-Std M1913 Picatinny rail measuring over 16 inches in length, even with the tiny 12.5-inch barreled version.

- The lower receiver has a heavily reinforced and deeply beveled magazine well and an ambidextrous bolt drop mechanism. With the positioning of the bolt release directly above the magazine release, the operator can empty a magazine, drop the empty magazine, insert a new magazine and drop the bolt to recharge the rifle, all without breaking the cheek-weld or taking the right hand off the pistol grip.

- The POF-USA C.R.O.S. system is the same as used in the 5.56mm rifles and will serve to enhance the function, performance, durability, and duration the P-308 will function for. With little to no carbon build-up due to the piston-driven operating system, combined with the silicone nickel coating on all major moving components, the reliability factor is levels above a traditional system. The P-308 utilizes the addition of the new NP3 Finish and will eventually replace the original as the C.R.O.S. Plus.

- The largest physical change may be the least visible without close inspection. The trigger group had been designed to meet the exact dimensions of all the guns in the .223 rifle series. This means all of the original existing trigger system's components and parts are interchangeable with the POF-USA P-308. All the new adjustable triggers and even the latest drop-in trigger systems can be used with the P-308, greatly increasing the gun's versatility.

Built Tough

Since the current primary operating environment for US battle rifles tends to be in hot, desert environments, the P-308 has been designed to combat the adverse effects of both heat and sand while requiring little downtime for standard maintenance when the necessity for a working rifle is the greatest.

Several factors have gone into increasing the reliability without major weight increases. The barrels are built from 4150 Mil-B-1159F Vanadium alloy with heavy machine gun fire in mind. Without sacrificing accuracy, if heavy fire is necessary the operator doesn't need to worry about overheating or overworking the barrel as much as with a standard barrel. Optional 5R Polygonal barrels can also be purchased. These barrels are case hardened and heat treated to 70 Rockwell, twice the hardness of mil-spec and hammer forged barrels. All barrels are threaded 5/8x24 and provided with the BC-A5 muzzle brake.

The bolt carrier key is integral to the billet machined steel bolt carrier, not an "add-on" part. The bolt carrier and the bolt are heat-treated and chrome plated.

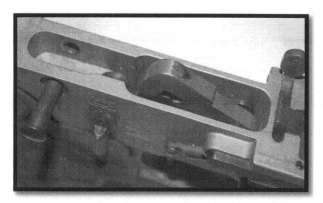

The fire control group has been designed to the exact specifications of a standard AR-15/M16/M4, allowing the user to utilize any of the numerous upgraded trigger systems available for that popular weapon system.

Both the upper and lower receivers are machined from 7075 T-6 aircraft aluminum alloy. The upper receiver is a Modular Railed Receiver (MRR) with a continuous monolithic top rail extending from the gas block to the charging handle. The upper receiver is coated on the interior with silicone nickel and the standard exterior finish on both receivers is black hard-coat anodized. The receiver and muzzle brake of our test rifle is finished with the Robar NP3 finish giving the receiver a non-reflective grey appearance. The black and grey combination lean more towards the "Urban Camo" style when compared to other finishes.

Magazine Compatibility

The POF-USA was manufactured to utilize a common .308 magazine rather than designing a new proprietary feeding device. After testing several systems, the decision was made to go back to the beginning of the big-bore black rifles and use the original ArmaLite AR-10 magazine design. This means you can use the following magazines with the P-308:

- Original (Waffle-Type) ArmaLite AR-10 magazines

- Knight SR-25 magazines

- DPMS Steel and Composite magazines

- POF-USA 25-round steel magazines

- C-Products 20-round stainless steel magazines

POF-USA Piston Operating System

Just like the POF-USA P-415 and P-416 rifle systems, the P-308 uses a gas piston mechanism instead of the direct gas impingement system. While the basic mechanism remains the same, a few parts are eliminated from the direct gas impingement system and are replaced with only three different parts to compose the piston system. The parts removed; the gas tube, the gas key and the gas rings include the parts that carry the hot gasses and excess carbon back inside the fire control mechanism and add greatly to the buildup of the material responsible for malfunction over prolonged use. With the POF-USA piston system, the gas rings are completely eliminated since they are no longer necessary for the system to function. This greatly decreases friction between the bolt and the bolt carrier making the mechanism much easier to cycle. A gas plug, gas piston and an operating rod and added and the system is complete. The gas plug has two positions: one for use with the rifle as shipped, and the second position is used in conjunction with a sound suppressor. This second position decreases the amount of gas volume used due to the additional backpressure created when using a sound suppressor. This combats excess recoil, gas blowback and an unwarranted rate of fire increase while suppressed. A simple 180-degree rotation is all that is necessary to change the gas plug position.

Trigger Time

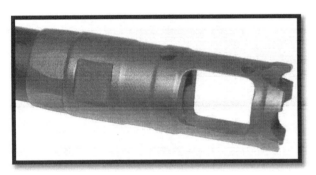

The BC-A5 muzzle device's contact points give it a unique look and aid in functions such as breaking glass while lessening the possibility of barrel damage.

Two things immediately come to mind when mentioning a 12-inch barrel and rifle cartridge in the same sentence: accuracy and muzzle velocity. Both were tested on a sub-freezing day in central Maine. Since it was unlikely that the mercury would rise any higher in the following weeks, a decision was made to conduct the testing in these frigid conditions, hovering around 0°F, often falling into the negative numbers. The average temperature for all shooting was only 5°F.

Because there was over 3 feet of snow on the ground with no sign of thaw for a few more months, our standard rifle ranges could not be utilized for these tests so an improvised range was established. A portable bench was set-up and standard B-27 silhouette targets were deployed at 100 yards and 200 yards with the assistance of a Bushnell laser rangefinder.

Accuracy Testing

Shooting for accuracy was the first order of the day and the P-308 system was topped with a BW Optic Y-TAC scope for this phase of testing. Targets were engaged at both 100 yards and 200 yards and 5-shot groups were recorded at each distance with 5 different types of ammo. We feel that the groups were quite "lose" compared to their real potential given the temporary range conditions and frigid temperatures. Retesting will be conducted at a later date to test this theory.

Ammo tested included Lake City M118 Special Ball 173gr. (FMJ), Federal Gold Medal 168gr. (BTHP), Wolf Gold 150gr. (SP), Remington Match 168gr. (HPBT) and Wolf Performance Ammunition 150gr. (FMJ). The tightest groups at 100 yards were fired with the Federal Gold Medal and the Remington Match. Both types gave us 4-shot groups under 1.25 inches but when the first "cold round" was factored in, the groups both measured just larger than 3 inches. Next was the Lake City with a 4-shot group of just under 1.5 inches and when factoring in the first "cold round" the 5-shot group came in at 2.85 inches. The Wolf Gold put 4 rounds in just under 2.25 inches and when adding the first "cold round" increased to 2.9 inches. The Wolf Performance Ammunition came in at 3.6 inches for the 4-round group and measured 4.25 inches when adding the initial "cold round."

Testing was duplicated at 200 yards with the following results; (Since we explained the "cold round" effect in the last paragraph but don't have enough solid data to know exactly who much difference it makes and how repeatable it is we will just report on the 5-shot group measurement this time). Wolf Performance Ammunition measured 3.4 inches, Wolf Gold grouped at 3.5 inches, Lake City was 3.6 inches, Federal Gold Medal measured 3.7 inches and the Remington Match came in at 4.1 inches.

Once again, it can't be stressed enough that the above numbers were recorded in less than ideal conditions. Shooting in sub-freezing temperatures, while wearing bulky clothing and walking through thigh-deep snow to tend targets will produce much different results than shooting on a covered range in the summer months. We hope these results may be valuable to those who work in these very cold environments and we also hope they are not directly compared to test results acquired in a controlled climate because they will not be equal.

Muzzle Velocity

The same ammunition used in the accuracy testing was also used to measure the muzzle velocity. The barrel of the test gun is a 12-inch barrel, rifled 1 turn in 10 inches and utilized a POF-USA BC-A5 muzzle brake. Since it was getting into a fairly low light situation in the last afternoon we had the opportunity to evaluate the ammo for visible flash. We found that the Wolf Performance Ammunition had the most flash, several times more than the others, and the Remington Match ammunition was a very distant second. We didn't do any shooting without the muzzle brake but by the absence of any major flash in the other loads we can assume it was effective. (It will be tested in a future issue of Small Arms Review in an article pertaining to the effectiveness of different muzzle brakes, flash hiders and other muzzle devices). The muzzle rise seemed minimal but the noise was quite noticeable. This brake combined with such a short barrel produced a sharp noise noticed by all shooters.

Due to the low lighting, a PACT MK IV XP Championship Timer & Chronograph was used in conjunction with the latest M6 Infrared Skyscreen kit. These screens use infrared lights and reflectors creating an accurate and useful "beam" for use in any lighting condition. At the time we finished the testing this day it was so dark it was difficult to see the impact area through the scope and the data just continued to roll in as though it was done in bright light. All measurements were recorded at 8 feet from the muzzle with an average temperature of 5°F.

The highest average muzzle velocity (MV) was recorded shooting the Wolf Performance Ammunition at 2,335 fps. It was followed by the Lake City M118 Special Ball at 2,239 fps, the Federal Gold Medal at 2,225 fps, the Wolf Gold at 2,221 fps and the Remington Match at 2,202 fps.

Almost all ammo was very consistent with the extreme spread over 5-shot strings recorded as follows: Wolf Gold - 29 fps, Wolf Performance Ammunition - 36 fps, Federal Gold Medal - 50 fps, Remington Match - 54 fps and Lake City M118 Special Ball - 130 fps.

Fit, Finish and Function

From first handling, it is apparent that the P-308 is manufactured with quality in mind. Everything is tight and solid. Frank DeSomma, CEO of POF-USA, has been prioritizing quality over quantity as long as this writer can remember and the P-308 is no exception. The details are in the "extras" that are available with the constantly evolving POF-USA product line. Some of these enhancements would include the machined, enlarged trigger guard over less expensive "snap-in" guards, and the ambidextrous bolt drop, designed and included at a significant additional production cost. The POF-USA "heat-sink" barrel nut is another example of using superior products in the production process rather than using less expensive, less effective parts that are readily available.

The finish on this particular rifle is the Robar NP3 Electroless Nickel on the receiver and the muzzle brake. The finish is extremely hard and resistant to corrosion and used in the Aerospace industry. The rail system is hard-coat anodized and the interior of the upper receiver, the charging handle, the bolt and carrier are all coated using the C.R.O.S. Plus system.

The function of the P308 will not disappoint. We found no particular ammo it didn't like and the adjustable gas plug is quickly rotated and positioned for suppressor use or heavy ammo. The short barrel on this particular test rifle provides a little more muzzle blast than one may be accustomed too but if you are a "short barreled rifle person" that is part of the allure. A little heavier than the much smaller P-415, it is also a heavyweight in performance making the additional weight a fair trade.

American Made

In these days of outsourcing for cheap parts and/or labor, you have to be cautious about the wording of manufacturing claims. "Assembled in the USA" usually has underlying meanings, as do several other tricky slogans. When we asked Frank DeSomma about his "Made in the USA" claim, he couldn't have been clearer and he proudly reiterates the following to anyone who will ask and on his website:

- All raw materials are manufactured from US Steel Mills.

- All heat treats, plating/coatings, are completed by U.S.A. owned and operated manufacturers.

- All accessory and component parts on our weapons systems are from U.S.A. owned and operated manufacturers.

- All POF-USA weapon systems are 100% pure American made.

Field Strip

The POF-USA P-308 disassembles exactly like the P-415 and P-416 5.56x45mm variants. The lower receiver is no different than the AR-15/M16/M4 family of firearms with the exception of the addition of the ambidextrous bolt release on the right side of the lower receiver. No tools are necessary to perform this procedure. Remove the magazine and make sure the firearm is unloaded by visually checking the chamber. Close the bolt carrier by depressing the bolt release. From the left side of the gun push both receiver pins to the right, through the receiver and pull them to the right until they stop. Remove the upper receiver from the lower receiver by lifting strait off. Gently pull the charging handle rearward and remove the bolt carrier from the rear. When the charging handle is all the way to the rear lower it inside the upper receiver to disengage it from the slot it rides in and remove from the rear. Depress the spring-loaded push pin on the gas plug and rotate the gas plug clockwise 45 degrees. (If the gas plug turns hard you can use the base of a .308 cartridge to assist it by inserting the rim into the gas plug groove.) Remove the gas plug by pulling to the front. Lower the muzzle and the gas piston, followed by the op-rod will slide out the hole opened by removing the gas plug. The rifle is field stripped and most cleaning and maintenance can be performed at this point. Reassemble the rifle in the reverse order.

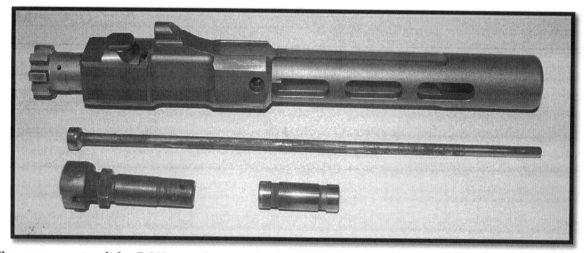

The components of the P-308 gas piston system: the gas plug, gas piston, push rod and bolt carrier. Note the he lightning cuts in the solid-machined bolt carrier to reduce weight while retaining strength.

Compatibility

While doing research for the P-308 article an item came to our attention that allows the weapon system to be even a little more universal. Cold War Shooters sells a pin sleeve that makes the POF-USA P-308 lower receiver compatible with the DPMS and Fulton .308 upper receivers. The sleeve is $19.50 and the model is simply: "POF.308Sleeve". Their website is: www.coldwarshoters.net.

Conclusion

The small package of a PDW with the knockdown power and distance capabilities of a much larger rifle is a homerun. Redesigning the lower receiver to accept all standard AR-15 trigger parts is a great leap forward due to the number of extremely high-quality aftermarket accessories available. Even though we didn't get the opportunity as of this writing to spend any meaningful time with this system as a suppressed platform, we have plans for it in the near future. Longer barrels are not always a good combination with subsonic ammunition due to increased friction over a longer surface area. We are thinking that this 12-inch barrel combined with a sound suppressor and a quality subsonic load may have some serious applications, especially when combined with the adjustable gas plug and a scope designed for multiple aiming points. Even though we have several ideas for future testing that we have not had time to complete yet, on our initial evaluation the POF-USA P-308 has all the earmarks of a winner.

The P-308 is available with a 14.5-inch barrel and permanently attached brake (bringing the legal barrel length to over 16 inches), a 16.5-inch barrel and even a 20-inch barrel if you would rather stay with a regular Title I firearm. At SAR we always opt for the NFA firearm to bring you the unique perspective you are unlikely to get in most other places. Regardless of your preferred barrel length, if you decide you would like to make the transition to a .308 in the familiar Black Rifle platform, you will not be disappointed with a P-308. To be completely fair, you may have just stumbled onto a new obsession.

The suggested retail price for any of the standard P-308 weapon systems is $2,500 and the lead-time at this printing was approximately 6 months.

POF-USA P-308 Technical Specifications (as tested)	
Caliber:	.308 Winchester (7.62x51 mm NATO)
Weight:	8 pounds, 11 ounces
Overall Length:	30.5 inches
Barrel Length:	12 inches
Barrel Material:	4150 Mil-B-1159F Vanadium Alloy
Rifling:	6-groove, 1 in 10 inches
Lower Receiver:	Billet machined 7075 T-6 aluminum

Upper Receiver:	Modular railed receiver 7075 T-6 aluminum
Trigger:	4-pound single-stage Timney drop-in group
Stock:	Vltor 6-position collapsible
Finish:	Robar NP3 electroless nickel

Brass Knuckles for the Black Rifle: The .450 Bushmaster

Hornady ammo is supporting the .450 Bushmaster rifle with a commercial load. It is accurate and consistent and gives the AR-15/M16 platform sufficient knockdown power for any game in North America.

With traditional bullet weights ranging from 55 to 62 grains, the AR-15/M16 weapon system is an impressive workhorse with a long history of service. Even though it has been the primary United States infantry weapon for over 40 years, the small 5.56x45mm round has been the subject of controversy for decades, sworn at by some and sworn by, by others. Regardless of your personal opinion of the Black rifle in the past, when you chamber this popular system with a 250-grain bullet with a muzzle velocity of 2,200 feet per second, you may have an entirely new outlook on it.

Introduced late in 2007, the .450 Bushmaster is the brainchild of Bushmaster Firearms and enjoys a cooperative effort with Hornady Ammunition. This new round is adapted from a 6.5mm (.284) case necked off to accept a Hornady (.452-inch diameter) 250-grain SST bullet. Manufactured to the same length as a standard .223 round, it is fed with a very similar box magazine fitted with a new single-stack follower. (The new follower is necessary because of the increased diameter of the case). As a tribute to a vision of Col. Jeff Cooper who often referred to a large diameter, fast moving round, the .450 Bushmaster has been nicknamed the "Thumper." With an impressive 2,800 foot-pounds of energy at the muzzle, it certainly seems fitting.

SAR received 2 variations to test for this article. The .450 Rifle has a 20-inch barrel and the .450 Carbine has a 16-inch barrel. Both barrels are ChroMoly Steel with Chrome lined chambers and bores and both utilize a right-hand twist with 1 turn in 24 inches to stabilize the heavy projectile. Both rifles are standard with an A3 Flat-Top upper receiver and free-floating aluminum handguard.

For the accuracy portion of our testing, the test rifle was topped with a BW Optic Y-TAC Scope and the carbine was fitted with a Leupold M8 Tactical scope.

Range Time

Tested on a sunny winter day, the mercury topped off around 45 degrees above zero. Targets were set at 100 yards and after a brief sighting-in period, the muzzle velocity of each variant was measured. According to the loading data on the Hornady box, the massive 250-grain projectile is supposed to be traveling 2,200 feet per second (fps) from a 20-inch barrel. We can confirm that Hornady did their homework as we recorded an average muzzle velocity of 2,203 fps. As expected, the carbine, with the 16-inch barrel, came in a little lower with an average of 1,705 fps. According to the manufacturers data the muzzle energy from the 20-inch barrel is an impressive 2,700 foot-pounds.

The muzzle velocity testing was almost an expected result based on our previous outings with Hornady ammo. They are often extremely accurate in their performance data, and proved once again to be on target.

The rifle and ammo accuracy was something we were quite anxious to test. After all, you can push a big bullet fast, but if you can't stabilize it and place it where you intend to, it doesn't provide a very useful tool. With the test rifles sighted in with their perspective glass, it was time to check the performance of the overall system. The first gun tested was the 20-inch rifle with the BW Optic Y-TAC scope. 5 rounds were fired within a 2-minute period, taking plenty of time to examine the previous hit and readjust cheek weld. (The beauty of making such big holes is they are extremely visible at 100 yards with nominal scope power). This first group fired barely reached 1.5 inches at its maximum spread. This type of accuracy was consistent throughout the entire shooting session.

The second test was with the 16-inch barreled carbine combined with the Leupold M8 Tactical Scope. 5 rounds were fired in the same manner as with the rifle version with even better results. This first group with the carbine barely broke the 1.25-inch mark at maximum spread. Once again, continued shooting remained consistent and just as tight through the remainder of the afternoon.

Thump!

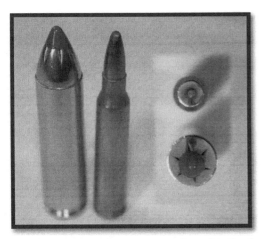

A comparison of the 250-grain .450 Bushmaster round and a 63-grain 5.56x45 Ultra Stealth round from Engel Ballistic Research.

The Bushmaster .450 is nicknamed "Thumper" for all the reasons pointed out above with the addition of one more. This rifle has a type of recoil that can only be described as a "thump." The first time the rifle was placed on the bench and the trigger slowly squeezed during the sighting in process, the author was reminded it was not a .223 rifle. As the scope gently kissed the top of the shooting glasses, a quick smile and a tighter hold followed through the remainder of the accuracy testing. No more lax, light holds on this rifle. At least not until it was time to shoot off-hand through the screens for some muzzle velocity testing. The first off-hand shot had exactly the same effect as the first bench shot and from this point on it wasn't repeated again.

Before you get too concerned about excessive recoil, it is really not severe at all. It just isn't a light .223. Neither gentle "tap" on the author's glasses had any adverse effect nor left any mark. Even though it is a big, heavy round traveling very fast, the traditional direct gas impingement system combined with an effective buffer keep the recoil manageable. It is not a severe "snap" or "crack", but more of a "push" like you would get from a medium gauge shotgun.

Conclusion

Given the number of people who typically believe "bigger is better" when it comes to stopping power, it would be hard to dislike this rifle system. Bushmaster and Hornady have made terrific partners in this joint effort as evidenced by the accuracy and consistency of this system. The load data was spot-on with our test data, and that indicates a serious amount of R&D on the part of all parties. The cost of ammo is not "crazy money" at a suggested retail (Hornady MSRP) of $37 per 20-round box either. It is not exactly surplus priced but it is not the kind of gun most would be firing a thousand rounds over a weekend. The recoil, while greater than the little .223 is very manageable and light enough for the author to comfortably fire several boxes of ammo in one setting.

Most parts of the .450 Bushmaster are "off the shelf" parts making the system a little more attractive to the tinkerers in our community. The trigger mechanism is standard as is the buffer system and spring. Most rail systems should work as long as the clearance issue is taken into consideration. The carbine used a standard front sight/gas block combination so anything is a go there. The rifle uses a low profile gas block and that is where the additional clearance will be a factor. The bolt carrier is the same as the others. While it was considered to swap it out for a full auto carrier and dropping in a registered lower, the 5-round magazine capacity was the main reason for forgoing this test. Keep an eye out for future magazine projects in the future but, for now, they are all only 5 rounds.

Both rifles were inspected and fired as they were shipped with no additional care or lube. Neither firearm malfunctioned in any way. After spending several hours with this combination it has already become apparent that the author will continue testing, right through the next season on Whitetail deer. If you are a fan of the Black Rifle and want to expand into a heavier caliber with high- grade performance, the .450 Bushmaster will not disappoint. It is quite impressive.

.450 Bushmaster Specifications	
Caliber:	.450 Bushmaster
Ammo:	250-Grain Hornady SST Flex Tip
Barrel:	ChroMoly Steel, right-hand twist, rifled 1 turn in 24 inches (1 in 609mm). Chrome lined bore and chamber. 16-inch (406mm) or 20-inch (508mm) lengths available
Overall Length:	Rifle – 39.25" (996 mm); Carbine 32.25" (895mm)
Weight (Unloaded):	Rifle – 8.13 pounds (230 gr) with BW Optic Y-TAC Scope; Carbine – 8.03 pounds (227 gr) with Leupold M8 Tactical Scope
Magazine Weight:	Unloaded – 4 ounces (113.3 gr); Loaded – 16 ounces (453.2 gr)
Sights (as shipped):	None. A3 "Flat Top" upper receiver with 1913 Mil-Std Picatinny rail to accept numerous sight options
Method of Operation:	Direct gas impingement, semiautomatic
Price:	Rifle - $1,350 MSRP; Carbine - $1,340 MSRP

We hope you enjoyed reading this book.

Follow Jeff Zimba on Facebook at:

www.facebook.com/Guntestvids

or on YouTube at:

www.youtube.com/bigshooterist

Watch for future titles from Jeff Zimba and other authors by visiting:

www.PrepperPress.com

Made in the USA
Middletown, DE
16 August 2015